I'VE LEARNED SOME THINGS

Modern Middle East Literatures in Translation Series

I'VE LEARNED SOME THINGS
SELECTED POEMS

ATAOL BEHRAMOĞLU

Translated by
WALTER G. ANDREWS

Introduction by
LAURENT MIGNON

The Center for Middle Eastern Studies
The University of Texas at Austin

Copyright © 2008 by the Center for Middle Eastern Studies at
The University of Texas at Austin.

Front cover photograph: *Turkish Market*, Wendy E. Moore
Back cover photographs: *Turkish Sky*, Wendy E. Moore
Detail, carved wooden door, Yeşil Türbe, Bursa, Christopher Rose
Cover and text design: Kristi Shuey
Series editor: Wendy E. Moore

Library of Congress Control Number: 2008932932
ISBN: 978-0-292-71969-9

The publication of this book was supported in part by a grant from the
Turkish Ministry of Culture and Tourism.

The translations in this book are based on the following
publications of Ataol Behramoğlu's work, from which the original
texts are also taken:

> *Bir Gün Mutlaka*, Istanbul: Epsilon (12th printing), 2006.
> *Yaşadıklarımdan Öğrendiğim Bir Şey Var*, Istanbul: Epsilon
> (13th printing), 2006.
> *Kızıma Mektuplar*, Istanbul: Epsilon (9th printing), 2006.
> *Sevgilimsin*, Istanbul: Epsilon (9th printing), 2006.
> *Aşk İki Kişiliktir*, Istanbul: Epsilon (5th printing), 2006.
> *Yeni Aşka Gazel*, Istanbul: Epsilon (2nd printing), 2006.

TABLE OF CONTENTS

III TURKEY, MY UNHAPPY LAND, MY LOVELY LAND

TRANSLATOR'S PREFACE

WALTER G. ANDREWS

I think of myself as an Ottomanist—a scholar specializing in the poetry of the Ottoman Empire in the fifteenth and sixteenth centuries—and not as a translator of modern Turkish literature. However, when I was asked, years ago, by a friend (Prof. Kemal Silay) to translate some modern Turkish poetry for his anthology, I agreed and found myself drawn into a fascinating, exciting, and entirely unexpected adventure. What began as an amusing diversion has grown into two books of translation and immensely rewarding personal relationships with two quite different poets, each a powerful artist in his own very special way. The Ottoman poets I have worked with for most of my career have been deceased for anywhere from one to six centuries. My relations with them are exclusively conjectural and I seldom need to take their opinions into account, and then only in a very abstract way. So working with very vital, intelligent, and engaged poets has been new for me, at once thrilling and intimidating.

My translations of Ataol Behramoğlu's poetry are not really mine alone. They are the product of a joint effort, of conversations, notes, letters, struggles, and a certain amount of whining on the part of the translator about the impossibility of doing what the poet wanted done. Behramoğlu's poetry is grounded in the simple and straightforward speech of everyday life, yet it also bears a significant burden of rhyme, assonance, and rhythm. Formally realized elements of sound are important to him. As can be seen from the original poems, most of his poems rhyme and he would have liked the translations to rhyme similarly. This did not always happen for reasons that seem worth mentioning. Because Turkish is an agglutinating language—which means that it creates vocabulary and grammar by adding elements to the ends of roots or words—it has many available rhymes, far more even than English, which has a larger overall active vocabulary. In my translations, I have valued the simplicity and clarity of Behramoğlu's poetry over the need for rhymes, and resisted torturing English syntax or sense to come up with close matches for the rhyme schemes of his originals. Translation is always a compromise and readers who know Turkish well will see places where we departed significantly or in minor ways from the original poems. In a sense, there are some poems that are really English versions—what Behramoğlu might have written had he been writing in English—rather than "close" translations. However, I always had the last word, so any mistakes or infelicities are my responsibility.

There are several people whose help and advice were crucial to this book. Unlike me, Laurent Mignon is an expert on modern Turkish literature and I feel very fortunate that he agreed to write an introductory essay for this volume. I am also grateful to Didem Gamze Erdinç, an excellent translator herself, who made many useful suggestions and corrections, and to my colleague at the University of Washington, Selim Kuru, who has always been available to help. In addition, I owe a large debt of gratitude to another expert on modern Turkish literature, Prof. Sibel Erol, who gave the manuscript a meticulous reading and made many significant suggestions for improvement. I am also indebted to Alphan Akgül for his help with the chronology of modern Turkish poetry.

Ataol Behramoğlu and I are also extremely grateful to Wendy Moore, Publications Editor for the Center for Middle Eastern Studies at the University of Texas. She not only accepted our translations for publication—which we think showed exceptional wisdom—but did an outstanding job of editing the final copy as well. Many thanks also to the designer, Kristi Shuey, who made our book lovely to look at.

INTRODUCTION:

A POET IN DIALOGUE WITH THE WORLD

LAURENT MIGNON

Skimming the pages of *Lotus*, the now defunct magazine of the Afro-Asian Writers' Association published in Arabic, English, and French, one comes across names such as Chinua Achebe, Mahmoud Darwish, Faiz Ahmed Faiz, and António Jacinto, names which have marked the history of world literature and become synonyms for writing that is both engaged and engaging. The Turkish poet Ataol Behramoğlu was awarded the Lotus literature prize in 1981 for his achievements. By then he had published not less than seven poetry collections, which had established him as Nâzım Hikmet's main heir: in other words, as an advocate of a socially engaged and revolutionary poetry that does not hold back from exploring even the most intimate realms of human experience. In a critique published the same year, Behramoğlu argued that the role of poetry was "to defend truth, humaneness, healthfulness and beauty against the lies spread through the mass media by imperialism and the false and fake sensitivities it creates."[1] Like many Turkish intellectuals for whom poetics had to rhyme with politics, he paid a harsh price for his socialist and pacifist convictions. In the dark years that followed the 1980 military coup, Behramoğlu was imprisoned for eleven months during the trial of the Turkish Peace Society, a non-governmental organization that militated for world peace and disarmament.

Ataol Behramoğlu's biography is a testimony to his internationalist engagement, which subverts both cultural borders in Turkey and political borders in the world. He was born in Çatalca, a district of Istanbul, on April 13, 1942, and because of his father's changing appointments as an agricultural engineer, spent his childhood in various places in Turkey, including Kars, well known to Orhan Pamuk readers, and the central Anatolian town of Çankırı. Behramoğlu studied Russian literature and graduated from Ankara University in 1966, one year after the publication of his first poetry collection, *Bir Ermeni General* (An Armenian General). In 1962, while he was a student, he joined the Turkish Workers' Party and accepted various responsibilities in this young political organization. His next collection, *Bir Gün Mutlaka* (One Day Surely), published in 1969, became a milestone of Turkish socialist poetry. Throughout the sixties and seventies he edited various influential, yet ephemeral, socialist culture magazines such as *Halkın Dostları* (The Friends of the People), which he published with fellow poet İsmet Özel, and *Militan* (The Militant), edited with his brother Nihat Behram, himself an acclaimed poet and novelist. Behramoğlu was also one of the founders of *Sanat Emeği* (The Labor of Art), an influential socialist monthly. During the early seventies, he lived in London, Paris, and Moscow, where he conducted research on Russian literature at Moscow State University. Returning to Turkey in 1974, he joined the Turkish State Theatres as a dramaturge. However, like many socialists, he was persecuted after the military coup in 1980. His most recent collection at the time, *Ne Yağmur . . . Ne Şiirler . . .* (Neither Rain . . . Nor Poems . . .), was seized and destroyed by the junta. To avoid a harsh prison sentence, he left the country in 1984 and went to France, where he remained until his acquittal in 1989. During his Paris years, Behramoğlu edited the journal *Anka*, a literary publication in French focusing on Turkish literature, and completed a PhD at the Sorbonne on the comparative poetics of Nâzım Hikmet and Vladimir Mayakovsky. Upon his return to Turkey, he was twice elected president of the Turkish Writers' Union.

Passionate love and political struggle are probably the two key aspects of his poetry. In a column written about these two concepts—*sevda* and *kavga*, as they are called in Turkish—

Behramoğlu situates his own poetry in the tradition of Western engaged, mainly socialist, poetry:

> You cannot dissociate love and struggle. There have been innumerable examples [of this association] throughout our century, in particular, in the works of distinguished poets such as Neruda, Nâzım [Hikmet], Mayakovski, Eluard and Aragon. What can be more natural than human beings who experience struggle and love organically, reflecting them jointly in their poems and songs?[2]

Thus it is not surprising that there should be intertextual relations between Behramoğlu's poetry and the works of the above-mentioned poets. The verse from "I've Learned Some Things," "To your utmost, listen to every beautiful song" (İnsan bütün güzel müzikleri dinlemeli alabildiğine), is like a response to Louis Aragon's verse "When music is beautiful, all human beings are equal" (Quand la musique est belle, tous les hommes sont égaux) from the poem "Complaint of Pablo Neruda" (Complainte de Pablo Neruda).[3] The principles of freedom, equality, and brotherhood achieved through art or even more revolutionary means are central to Behramoğlu's understanding of socialism.

Four generations of Turkish poets can be classified as socialist poets. However, socialist poetry and socialist literature are controversial literary classifications in Turkey, just like anywhere else, because none of the founding fathers of socialism had a clear idea on the role of socialist literature. Karl Marx and Friedrich Engels did not develop any comprehensive system of literary theory. Their scattered writings on literature and the arts were only collected and published in 1933 by M. Lifshitz and F. P. Schiller, and this collection did not became widely known until after the Second World War. There have been, ever since, great divergences among leading Marxist thinkers on the role of literature in the revolutionary struggle. Hence the affinity between the poets categorized as socialist is not necessarily literary but rather political, even though this latter point, too, can be a source of antagonism, since there is no love lost between the various components of the socialist left in Turkey.

Historically, Marxism as an ideology gained influence among the intelligentsia of Salonika and Istanbul during the first quarter of the twentieth century, and it rapidly became a major political force in literary cafés, though the emerging working class and the peasants in the Islamic lands of what remained of the Ottoman Empire were less responsive. Despite the young Turkish Republic's initially good relations with the Soviet Union and Mustafa Kemal's ambivalent attitude toward socialist ideology, the socialist movement was given little freedom to develop in Atatürk's time and was later persecuted by the authoritarian regime of İsmet İnönü. In this particular context, the aim of socialist literature was, in the words of the poet Rıfat Ilgaz (1911–1993), one of its major proponents, "to analyze the circumstances of the period with Marxist methodology, to share the findings with society and to find solutions in the framework of the constitution of the Turkish Republic."[4] In other words, literature was not only conceived of as a propaganda tool, but also as a possible way to analyze the workings of society.

Nâzım Hikmet (1902–1963) can rightly be seen as the father of Turkish socialist literature, even though some minor literary figures before him, like Yaşar Nezihe (1880–1935) and Rasim Haşmet (1884[?]–1918), had bridged the gap between the committed humanism of Tevfik Fikret (1867–1915) and the more ideological poetry of the late thirties. It was under the influence of Nâzım Hikmet that a whole generation started to write verses that called for a socialist revolution. They were to be known as the Generation of 1940 (1940 Kuşağı). Attilâ İlhan (1925–2005), a major left-wing poet and critic, referred to them "as a squad of self-sacrificing soldiers,"[5] by which he pointed to the ruthless suppression of socialist activism during the forties. Their poetry was characterized by an active socialist engagement and a radical rejection of tradition and of contemporary literary trends. It should be noted that their rejection of the classical and syllabist neo-folk traditions took place at a time when Nâzım Hikmet was working on a synthesis of modernist, traditional, and divân poetry. But the members of the Generation of 1940 could not be completely informed of Hikmet's new endeavors because his works were forbidden. Instead, they were mainly acquainted with his earlier futurist and constructivist experiments. The poetry of the Generation of 1940 led to greater realism and thus to a thematic development in Turkish poetry. While critics agree that the poetry itself is more interesting from a documentary perspective than from a literary one, they also point to the difficult circumstances in which the poets wrote. Socialist poets, whose ideas were outlawed, had to work under the constant gaze of the authorities and suffered continuous harassment. Nevertheless, the poetry of the Generation of 1940 does certainly compare favorably with the poetry of the neo-Parnassian Seven Torch Holders (Yedi Meşaleciler), and other contemporary trends inspired by neo-folk poetry or the avant-garde Garip (Bizarre). But unlike the conservative and nationalist versifiers, the first socialist poets were widely ignored by mainstream literary criticism and are hardly mentioned in works of literary historiography.

However, the Generation of 1940 facilitated the emergence of several poets who outgrew the narrow framework of Zhdanovist literature.[6] A new wave of socialist poetry developed during the sixties after the legalization of Nâzım Hikmet's works in 1965. A whole new generation of young poets, among them Ataol Behramoğlu, was introduced to the poetry of the *blue-eyed giant*. But situating Behramoğlu's poetry only in the context of Turkish and world socialist poetry is insufficient. The poet himself takes a critical stance toward the concept of socialist literature—more particularly toward socialist realism—and in that sense, too, he is a true heir to Nâzım Hikmet, whose approach to poetry was often criticized both at home and abroad by holders of a more dogmatic view of socialist realism.

Behramoğlu is a fierce critic of what he calls "mechanical socialism" (Mekanik toplumculuk) and has devoted several articles to its ills. As one of the founders and the editor of the monthly magazine *Halkın Dostları* (Friends of the People, 1970–1971), he criticized versifiers who equated socialist realism with merely focusing on the problems of the working class. In an article dating from 1970, he made a harsh assessment of the works of contemporary socialist poets:

> Most of our fellow poets believe that socialist poetry consists of writing about the oppression and the poverty of the people. This is a grave mistake. This attitude reflects a populist approach and a tendency to satisfy petty bourgeois cravings. There is no doubt that it is very noble to wish to write about the oppression of the people and about poverty. But socialist poetry cannot only be the poetry of complaint.[7]

Behramoğlu argues that socialist poetry should be poetry of resistance and revolt. It should not consist of a mere glorification of the people, but ought to reflect all the contradictions that can be found in the attitude of the working class.[8] He favors a critical realism that comprises every realm of human experience. He advocates what he calls "organic poetry" (*organik şiir*) and defines it in opposition to "synthetic," "artificial," and "mechanical" poetry. Organic poetry is "personal" (*kişisel*) but not "individualistic" (*bireyci*). It should not be constrained by extreme formalism but should evolve like a living organism in contact with the real world.[9] Such a definition opens up spaces for the articulation of more personal concerns and the exploration of intimate emotions, such as in the poem "I've Learned Some Things":

> You should know sorrow, honorably, with all your being
> Because the pains, like joys, make a person grow
> Your blood should mingle in the great circulation of life
> And in your veins, life's endless fresh blood should flow

Like many Turkish poets who started publishing in the sixties, Behramoğlu wrote at a critical yet inspirational time in the history of Turkish poetry: The poetry of Nâzım Hikmet was legally available and could be freely read and studied, maybe for the first time, and the avant-gardist trio Garip, lead by Orhan Veli (1914–1950), and the modernist Second Renewal (İkinci Yeni) had completely transformed the understanding of poetry, relegating both neoclassical and syllabic poetry to an outmoded past. Poetically, an infinity of new worlds could now be built. However, these two literary trends had, until then, been mercilessly condemned by most left-wing as well as conservative literati. Attilâ İlhan was particularly vocal in his critiques of Garip. In an article evocatively entitled "What a Shame for Turkish Poetry," he repeated the claim that Garip's apolitical poetry had been the official poetry of the İnönü regime.[10] This claim is not totally unsubstantiated since Garip had the support of Nurullah Ataç, an influential critic close to the regime. Ataç's and Garip's agendas overlapped. Ataç worked on a radical redefinition of Turkish culture, which he judged to be too Oriental, whereas Garip rejected both classical and folk literature, even claiming that they wanted to reinvent poetry. Indeed, the final sentence of their manifesto, which had been drawn up by Orhan Veli, went as far as arguing "one ought to be against everything that was ancient and above all against poeticality."[11] However, in the sixties, even though uninspired poets claiming Garip's heritage had proliferated, left-wing intellectuals were in a better position to judge the original achievements of the three founding writers: Garip's trademark was the rejection of every poetic convention. Ordinary life and emotions were central in their down-to-earth poetry that strove to describe subjective experiences and not objective realities. Moreover, they managed to establish the free verse as the meter of modern Turkish poetry, thus bringing the reign of the syllabic meter to an end. Socialist poets, too, had championed the free verse, but heavy censorship and political persecution had seriously impeded the dissemination of their works. Nonetheless, Garip's subjective realism was not that distant from the literary goals of socialist poets who, in Nâzım Hikmet's terms, aimed at representing both "the misery of mankind" and "personal tragedies."[12]

Some of Behramoğlu's early verses even have that slight surrealistic and humorous spirit suggestive of Orhan Veli or, indeed, of Jacques Prévert, with whom Veli shared a common poetic sensitivity. The 1961 poem "Cat" is a case in point:

> "Farewell, farewell" how nice is that
> A third one leaves the harmony flat
> "Farewell, farewell, farewell"
> What's more, it seems just like a cat

Behramoğlu's approach to the Second Renewal, the other trend that profoundly upset the Turkish poetic landscape, is similarly open-minded and critical. In the beginning the Second Renewal was a reaction against the general literary atmosphere in Turkey. The designation Second Renewal is misleading, though. At the time when the term was coined, critics had started to write about the Garip group as being the First Renewal. Hence one could erroneously conclude that the Second Renewal was the continuation of Garip. On the contrary, they rejected what they saw as the superficiality and the lack of depth of Garip poetry and of those who walked in the footsteps of the group. The Second Renewal also took a critical stance against the politically engaged poetry of the Generation of 1940 and later socialist poets. Their approach was elitist as they felt that the poetic language could not be a tool to convey a message, but only constituted the context in which the poet worked. Nonetheless, their stance was profoundly subversive and one could argue that their libertarian approach and focus on sexuality challenged the social status quo.

Though like most left-wing critics Behramoğlu was ill at ease with this elitist understanding of poetry, he acknowledged its influence on his generation at a time when this was far from being fashionable. In 1970, he wrote in an article published in *Devrim* (Revolution):

As a new generation of socialist writers, we have to understand and assimilate the constructive aspects of every kind of poetry past and present. [. . .] If we do not synthesize the positive qualities of the Second Renewal poets, we will have ignored a 15-year-old experience. We have to understand the characteristics and to assimilate the useful aspects of the Second Renewal but also of Ahmed Arif, Orhan Veli, the syllabists, Nâzım Hikmet, Yahya Kemal, the Tanzimat poets, divan and folk poetry, in other words not only of Turkish but also of world poetry.[13]

The above quotation substantiates Behramoğlu's nonsectarian approach to literature—an attitude that was unusual on the Far Left in the seventies—and his interest in world poetry. Indeed Behramoğlu, today a professor in Istanbul University's Department of Russian Language and Literature, is also an acclaimed translator who has translated some of the key figures in modern Russian literature, such as Alexander Pushkin, Mikhail Lermontov, Ivan Turgenev, Anton Chekhov, and Maxim Gorky. Moreover, he has edited, together with fellow poet Özdemir İnce, a four-volume anthology of world poetry that covers a wide and eclectic range of poets from the Angolan poet and former president Agostinho Neto to Stelios Geranis from Greece.

Since the modernizing reforms of the Tanzimat (1839–1876) and the subsequent growing interest in Western, mainly French, culture and literature, translation has continuously played a central role in Turkish literary, scientific, and academic life. It is one of the particularities of Turkish intellectual life that most major Turkish writers and poets have, until recently, also been translators. Key works of Western literature have been translated into Turkish by some of Turkey's foremost authors. The translation of Émile Zola's novel *Thérèse Raquin* by Muallim Naci, a leading poet and critic of the last quarter of the nineteenth century; the translation of Thomas

Mann's *Death in Venice* by the influential poet and critic Behçet Necatigil; and, more recently, the translation of selected poems by Ted Hughes, Philip Larkin, and Yehuda Amichai by Roni Margulies, the winner of the prestigious 2002 Yunus Nadi poetry prize, are just some examples of this phenomenon.

Nonetheless, it would be insufficient to explain Behramoğlu's activities as a translator only by referring to the Turkish intellectual's self-appointed role as an educator of the people and a bridge between cultures, or to his passion for poetry. The act of translating should also be interpreted in the context of Behramoğlu's internationalist engagement. Examples of his commitment to solidarity with the oppressed and his opposition to bourgeois nationalism abound in his theoretical texts and in his literary works. In the intensely emotional yet simple poem "Babies Don't Have Nations," he points to the obvious but rarely highlighted fact that newborn children share a common language:

> I felt this for the first time far from my homeland
> Babies don't have nations
> The way they hold their heads is the same
> They gaze with the same curiosity in their eyes
> When they cry, the tone of their voices is the same

Growing up thus becomes a reenactment of the unfortunate biblical event at Babel, the loss of the universal language. However, common tongues continue to subsist and Behramoğlu's poetry unearths them. In the poem "What Do the Greek Songs Say," the poet points to similarities between Greek and Turkish music, thus undermining nationalist discourses on the historical rivalry between Greece and Turkey:

> What do the Greek songs say
> Is it that all songs will one day be one
> What do the Greek songs say
> So distant . . . yet not so far away

Responses in Greek to such pacifist cravings do exist of course. The opening verses of "Peace" (Eirini), by Yannis Ritsos, could be read in parallel to Behramoğlu's poem. It should be noted that Behramoğlu translated this poem into Turkish.

> The dreams of a child are peace.
> The dreams of a mother are peace.
> The words of love under the trees,
> are peace.[14]

But Behramoğlu's quest for emotional and intellectual symbiosis goes far beyond modern Turkey's geographical borders. Hence in the poem "A Very Strange Black," the symbiotic relationship between the narrator and an unknown black man in Harlem becomes a symbol of the dignity and equality of all human beings:

> There, where Walt Whitman is from, a black
> In Harlem, its leaves after rain
> A glass of gin, double martini
> As if feeling my self there in the dark

The poem, dating from 1962, should also be read as a declaration of the poet's solidarity with the oppressed black minority in the United States at a time when the African-American civil rights movement was at its height. Behramoğlu's stance was far from being ordinary in Turkey. National-conservative intellectuals, such as Mehmet Çınarlı, the editor of the literary monthly *Hisar* (The Fortress), were inclined to reproduce and appropriate the white supremacist discourse in their own publications.[15]

Behramoğlu's internationalist viewpoint is confirmed by a web of literary references in his poems, either by directly mentioning the names of influential writers, philosophers, and poets such as Albert Camus ("How Awful When Poetry Ages as It Is Read"), Anton Chekhov ("August Guest"), René Descartes ("One Day Surely"), Mikhail Lermontov ("One

Day Surely"), Dylan Thomas ("With Dylan Thomas"), and Walt Whitman ("A Very Strange Black"), or through intertextual connections in poems such as "It Was Paris," a meditation, full of lament, evoking Apollinaire's "The Pont Mirabeau" (Le pont Mirabeau):

Compare, Behramoğlu:

> It was Paris, the Paris of what time
> Flying off with my fly-away life
> Suddenly everything turned to memory
> Love turned to lament

And Apollinaire:

> Under the pont Mirabeau flows the Seine
> Our loves flow too
> Must it recall them so
> Joy came to us always after pain[16]

> Sous le pont Mirabeau coule la Seine
> Et nos amours
> Faut-il qu'il m'en souvienne
> La joie venait toujours après la peine[17]

Another instance of intertextual connections can be found in "Babies Don't Have Nations," whose central strophes semantically and syntactically evoke the final verses of the Georgian poet Vazha Pshavela's poem "Tell the Lovely Violet." Behramoğlu writes:

> Fathers, do not let them slip your minds
> Mothers, protect your babies
> Silence them, silence them, don't let them speak
> Who would talk of war and destruction

Let us leave them to grow up with passion
May they sprout and burgeon like saplings
They are not yours, nor mine, nor anybody's
They belong to the whole world
They are the apple of all humanity's eye

And Pshavela in the same vein:

Let her not see the sun, she'll only regret it,
When she discovers it is not permanent!
Oh earth, to you consigned let
This my lovely violet remain,
Protect her, be a parent to her,
As is your custom.[18]

Though international literary references abound in his works, Ataol Behramoğlu's poetry is also about Turkey. However, the reader in search of Orientalist clichés will be looking for them in vain. Behramoğlu's Turkey is "lovely," yet "unhappy." Istanbul, of course, is an important theme in his poetry, but the focus of his verses is more on the ordinariness of the city than on the breathtaking skyline of its historical quarters. Its streets are "poor" and "unlit." The street sellers have "worn hands" ("Through Those Poor, Unlit Streets"). The poet chooses to focus on those aspects of the city that are usually ignored by postcard designers and Western travelers. But misery and poverty are universal realities. Behramoğlu's poetry is deeply humane and humanistic.

He challenges and undermines nationalist and idealist discourses on the representation of Turkey—in particular of the Anatolian mainland—in poetry, a major theme of literary criticism even today. During the first decades of the twentieth century, the Five Syllabists (Beş Hececiler), for instance, wanted to engage with the ordinary reality of Anatolian people in their works and sought to connect them to their nationalist project of self-definition. The imperial Ottoman past and cosmopolitan Istanbul were banished from, or at least condemned in, their verses. However, their depiction of Anatolia, novel though it was, had little to do with Anatolian realities since the Istanbul-based poets had almost no direct experience of Anatolian life. Their nationalist pastorals depicted a hypothetical state of felicity untainted by urban cosmopolitanism and modernity.

Behramoğlu's Anatolia has nothing in common with the bucolic verses of the Five Syllabists, which are still part of the very conservative literature curriculum for high schools. He writes about boredom in provincial towns and stresses the universality of this situation ("Evening Sorrow in Country Towns"):

> Evening sorrow in country towns
> It's the same the whole world over
> Clear blue sky and phantom houses
> And the sad glances of women

He takes the reader far away from the idyllic verses that narrate the love games of naive village girls and astute shepherds. In some poems, he subverts more directly the pastoral codes, as in the opening quatrain of "In Praise of Cows":

> In my life I've seen so many cows
> I must write for them a poem of praise
> Cows lounging, strewn about the meadows
> Cows endlessly musing as they graze

Though Behramoğlu parodies syllabist poetry—whose achievements he nonetheless acknowledges in his critical writings—he establishes a critical dialogue with the communist Hasan İzzettin Dinamo's (1909–1989) brand of pastoral poetry. Dinamo's pastoral poems were often targeted for reproach by fellow travelers from the Turkish Marxist left who believed in a more propagandist poetry. It is true that an uninformed reading of Dinamo's sonnets could lead to pastoral interpretations. However, read in the light of Hasan İzzettin Dinamo's experiences—imprisonment and torture—it becomes obvious that his poems are not literary attempts to preserve the political and social status quo, which is what pastoral poets implicitly aim at. The nostalgic evocation of the beloved and nature, of innocent games of love in idyllic conditions, is the expression of a deep craving for freedom:

Whenever you're on my mind I remember the *Green River*
Your fair face, your auburn hair, your immaculate dress
Slowly unveiled among the mist
In those gardens filled with fragrant apples[19]

In the opening lines of "Poem on the Threshold of Forty," Behramoğlu seems to oppose his own pantheist extolling of life to the dreamlike and static atmosphere of Dinamo's sonnets:

From these minor enthusiasms, time out
Because the sun is my brother
I'm making love with a river
Because I'm the same age as the wind

But Behramoğlu's emphasis on movement and energy, which is not without reminders to the reader of Walt Whitman's celebration of sexuality and nature, should not be read as a denigration of Dinamo's bucolic verses. The differences in the perception and representation of nature in these two poems emphasize the ordeal suffered by the political prisoner for whom nature has become a lost paradise, unchanging and ageless. It is one of Turkish literary history's terrible ironies that Behramoğlu was jailed one year after he wrote these verses.

Though Behramoğlu is quite critical of what could best be described as a Turkish version of Heimatliteratur and the idealization of rural life and traditions, his poetry is nonetheless deeply anchored in Turkish reality. He is only too conscious of the fact that the borderline between patriotism and jingoism is blurred and that the patriotic feelings of the people have, in the past as well as today, been hijacked to bury more concrete social and economic problems. He relates to Turkey on a more personal and emotional level in his poems. The poetry of ordinary life plays a central role in this approach in which subjective and trivial details find their way into his poetry and exemplify various facets of material reality, as can be seen in the poem "When Leaving Town":

> The things recalled when leaving town
> Are mostly little things
> The grocer's bill is paid
> At the last moment, one runs into a distant acquaintance

This aspect of his work resembles Orhan Veli's later poetry and Nâzım Hikmet's brand of subjective realism developed particularly in his love poems written for Pirâye in the thirties and forties.

Love is a central theme in the poetry of Ataol Behramoğlu. However, he rarely approaches this theme on its own, but instead discusses it in a wider social context. The real world, a world of social struggles, injustices, and individual tragedies, is the setting of love. In Behramoğlu's poetic universe, love is less an emotion than an action, and the act of lovemaking thus gains a symbolic significance, as in the opening verse of the poem "One Day Surely," written in 1965: "Today I made love and then I joined in a march" (Bugün seviştim, yürüyüşe katıldım sonra). The act of love and the protest march are expressions of the same need for action, for grasping and shaping reality. The link between love and political activism is, of course, one of the great themes of socialist poetry. Human solidarity as a natural extension of private love has been a theme used by poets such as Louis Aragon, Paul Eluard, and Nâzım Hikmet, who wrote that "life was not worth living unless one was in love with both one person and millions of people,"[20] a maxim Behramoğlu could easily appropriate. The loving couple in his poetry can be interpreted as the founding principle of a loving, peaceful, and humane society.

However, the universe of Ataol Behramoğlu's love poetry can also be uneasy. There are constant references to violence. In the lyrical poem "This Love Ends Here," which deals with the separation of two lovers, the contrast between the child, a symbol of innocence, and the weapon is striking. Childhood is an ever-occurring theme in Behramoğlu's poetry and symbolizes a craving for lost innocence. The narrator may still be a child in his heart, but his acts are those of a grown man. The fact that the narrator carries a weapon means that he may have to lose his innocence, and is an obvious reference to state repression and to the political violence that has shaped much of the experiences of the socialist left in republican Turkey:

> This love ends here and me . . . I'm up and gone
> Child in my heart, in my pocket a revolver
> This love ends here, have a good day, lover
> And me, I'm up and gone, a river flowing on

There is a striking discrepancy between the musicality of the poem and the harshness of the message conveyed. The repetition of rhymes in "–er" is not fortuitous in this poem on the border between lyric and political poetry. *Er* means soldier in Turkish. Similarly, in "You Are My Beloved," a later poem written in 1990, references to "youth bleeding," "unfinished lovemaking," and to the beloved's "wak[ing] in the night screaming" provide a subtext referring to a tough and violent background. It is not surprising that the narrator of the love poems occasionally yearns, full of despair, for his beloved "in the depths of annihilation" ("In Secret My Beloved").

The emphasis on sensuality and sexuality in several poems should be read both as an attempt to challenge the taboos concerning sexuality in Turkish society and as a way to underscore the materiality of love. By writing about lovemaking, Behramoğlu shares intimate moments with the reader, thus making the private public, as, for instance, in "The Erotic Gazel":

> Feet that I will cup in my palms
> Like a pair of white carnations
>
> Glances sparkling with desire
> Lips trembling with mystery

One could argue that Behramoğlu's poetry is poetry of demystification and focuses on the subjective perceptions of the narrator and on social realities. By stressing the materiality of poetry in, for instance, "How Awful When Poetry Ages as It Is Read," or the material context of literary creation, as in the poem "August Guest," he demystifies literature and thus challenges both elitist and idealist approaches to art:

> I was translating a Chekhov short story
> A glass of beer on my table
> —My room, my books, my ordinary world—
> On the tulle curtains the sunbeams of August

His latest poetry collection, *Gazel to a New Love*, with its strong erotic undertone and representations of lovemaking—the physical aspects of love—gains particular relevance in this attempt to explore and celebrate the materiality of life. The choice of the gazel—a short, more or less sonnet-length Ottoman love poem in which the "love" is often read today as purely metaphorical—is thus meaningful. The poet challenges the assumptions regarding the mystical nature of the gazel and presents his own materialist conception of love. Love is much more than a metaphor. This is reminiscent, of course, of Nâzım Hikmet's subversion of the mystical nature of *rubâis*, the quatrains of the classical tradition, by using them to explore his materialist conception of love.

At a time when some want us to believe in a conflict of civilizations between a mystical and irrational Orient and a materialist and Cartesian West, Ataol Behramoğlu's poetry is a powerful reminder that the world is much more complex. Indeed, Behramoğlu is a poet in dialogue with the real world. In a recent article where he wondered what Nâzım Hikmet's stance in the post-September 11 world would have been, Behramoğlu was probably describing his own standpoint too, thus directly challenging the prophets of the clash of civilizations:

> On whose side would Nâzım Hikmet have been after the catastrophe of September 11, 2001? Probably, on the side of the real world . . . As a humanist, Nâzım Hikmet would have felt true and deep sorrow for the thousands of innocent victims who lost their lives in the Twin Towers. He would have shared the pain of the American people (and of the world). But armed with his social conscience and anti-imperialist convictions, the same Nâzım Hikmet would have realized beforehand where things were going to end up. He would have made efforts to warn humanity about the real aims hidden behind the crocodile tears of imperialism [. . .].[21]

Notes

1. Ataol Behramoğlu, "Şiir, İnsancıllık, Yurtseverlik," *Şiirin Dili–Anadil* (Istanbul: Adam, 1995), 163.
2. Ataol Behramoğlu, "Sevda ve Kavga Sözleri," *Kimliğim: İnsan* (Istanbul: Cumhuriyet Kitapları, 2006), 52.
3. Louis Aragon, "Complainte de Pablo Neruda," *Oeuvres poétiques complètes I* (Paris: Gallimard, 2007), 1111.
4. Quoted in Metin Cengiz, *Toplumcu Gerçekçi Şiir 1923–1953* (Istanbul: Tümzamanlaryayıncılık, 2000), 13.
5. Attilâ İlhan, "O 'Fedailer' ki," *Hangi Edebiyat* (Ankara: Bilgi, 1993), 45.
6. Zhdanovism was the official cultural doctrine of the Soviet Union between 1946 and 1952 and aimed at eradicating supposedly apolitical, bourgeois, and individualistic literature.
7. Ataol Behramoğlu, "Toplumcu Şiir Üstüne Birkaç Söz," *Yaşayan bir Şiir* (Istanbul: Adam, 1993), 19.
8. Ibid., 19–20.
9. Ataol Behramoğlu, "Organik Şiir," *Yaşayan bir Şiir* (Istanbul: Adam, 1993), 104–106.
10. Attilâ İlhan, "Yazık Oldu Türk Şiirine," *Hangi Edebiyat* (Ankara: Bilgi, 1993), 260.
11. Orhan Veli, "Garip," *Bütün Şiirler* (Istanbul: Adam, 1999), 36.
12. Quoted in Aziz Çalışlar, ed., *Nâzım Hikmet: Sanat ve Edebiyat Üzerine Yazılar* (Istanbul: Bilim ve Sanat, 1987), 65.
13. Ataol Behramoğlu, "Nedir İkinci Yeni'den Geçmek?" *Yaşayan bir Şiir* (Istanbul: Adam, 1993), 13.
14. Yannis Ritsos, "Peace," in *Yannis Ritsos: Selected Poems 1938–1988*, trans. and ed. Kimon Friar and Kostas Myrsiades (Brockport: BOA Editions, 1989), 51.
15. See for instance, Mehmet Çınarlı, *Altmış Yılın Hikâyesi* (Istanbul: Kaknüs, 1999), 149.
16. Guillaume Apollinaire, *Selected Writings of Guillaume Apollinaire*, trans. Roger Shattuck (New York: New Directions Books, 1950), 65.
17. Guillaume Apollinaire, "Le pont Mirabeau," *Alcools* (Paris: Editions Gallimard, 1989), 15.
18. Vaja-Pshavela, "Tell the Lovely Violet," in *A Georgian Reader*, ed. George Hewitt (London: SOAS, 1996), 256.
19. Hasan İzzettin Dinamo, "Sonnet II," in *Son Yüzyıl Büyük Türk Şiiri Antolojisi 1*, ed. Ataol Behramoğlu (Istanbul: Sosyal, 1997), 246.
20. Nâzım Hikmet, *Bursa Cezaevinden Va-Nu'lara Mektuplar*, ed. Vala Nurettin (Istanbul: Cem, 1970), 57.
21. Ataol Behramoğlu, "Nâzım Kimden Yana Olurdu," *Kendin Olmak ya da Olmamak* (Istanbul: İnkılâp, 2003), 152.

I'VE LEARNED SOME THINGS

I'VE LEARNED SOME THINGS

I've learned some things from having lived:
If you're alive, experience one thing with all your power
Your beloved should be worn out from being kissed
And you should drop exhausted from the smelling of a flower

A person can gaze at the sky for hours
Can gaze for hours at a bird, a child, the sea
To live on the earth is to become part of it
To strike down roots that won't pull free

If you cling to anything, tightly hold a friend
Fight for something with every muscle, whole body, all your passion
And if you lay yourself for a time on the warm beach
Let yourself rest like a grain of sand, a leaf, a stone

To your utmost, listen to every beautiful song
As though filling all the self with sound and melody
One should plunge headfirst into life
As one dives from a cliff into the emerald sea

Distant lands should draw you, people you don't know
To read every book, know others' lives, you should be burning
Exchange nothing for a glass of water's joy
No matter how much the pleasure, fill your life with yearning

You should know sorrow, honorably, with all your being
Because the pains, like joys, make a person grow
Your blood should mingle in the great circulation of life
And in your veins, life's endless fresh blood should flow

YAŞADIKLARIMDAN ÖĞRENDİĞİM BİR ŞEY VAR

Yaşadıklarımdan öğrendiğim bir şey var:
Yaşadın mı, yoğunluğuna yaşayacaksın bir şeyi
Sevgilin bitkin kalmalı öpülmekten
Sen bitkin düşmelisin koklamaktan bir çiçeği

İnsan saatlerce bakabilir gökyüzüne
Denize saatlerce bakabilir, bir kuşa, bir çocuğa
Yaşamak yeryüzünde, onunla karışmaktır
Kopmaz kökler salmaktır oraya

Kucakladın mı sımsıkı kucaklayacaksın arkadaşını
Kavgaya tüm kaslarınla, gövdenle, tutkunla gireceksin
Ve uzandın mı bir kez sımsıcak kumlara
Bir kum tanesi gibi, bir yaprak gibi, bir taş gibi dinleneceksin

İnsan bütün güzel müzikleri dinlemeli alabildiğine
Hem de tüm benliği seslerle, ezgilerle dolarcasına
İnsan balıklama dalmalı içine hayatın
Bir kayadan zümrüt bir denize dalarcasına

Uzak ülkeler çekmeli seni, tanımadığın insanlar
Bütün kitapları okumak, bütün hayatları tanımak arzusuyla yanmalısın
Değişmemelisin hiç bir şeyle bir bardak su içmenin mutluluğunu
Fakat ne kadar sevinç varsa yaşamak özlemiyle dolmalısın

Ve kederi de yaşamalısın, namusluca, bütün benliğinle
Çünkü acılar da, sevinçler gibi olgunlaştırır insanı
Kanın karışmalı hayatın büyük dolaşımına
Dolaşmalı damarlarında hayatın sonsuz taze kanı

I've learned some things from having lived:
If you're alive, experience largely, merge with rivers,
        heavens, cosmos
For what we call living is a gift given to life
And life is a gift bestowed upon us

Yaşadıklarımdan öğrendiğim bir şey var:
Yaşadın mı büyük yaşayacaksın, ırmaklara, göğe, bütün evrene
    karışırcasına
Çünkü ömür dediğimiz şey, hayata sunulmuş bir armağandır
Ve hayat, sunulmuş bir armağandır insana

I   THIS LOVE ENDS HERE

ISTANBUL

I'm drawing an Istanbul on my breast
With my forefinger, butterfly-styled
Before the mirror as though I were a child
Face and hair I caress.

Of Kadıköy I recall some sort of seas
Of Shishli a solitary tram
Of Samatya, of Sultanahmet I am
Remembering the fig trees.

I'm drawing an Istanbul on my breast
With my forefinger, butterfly-styled
Look, I'm a little hopeless, a little tired
I think I like my eyes the best.

İSTANBUL

Göğsüme bir İstanbul çiziyorum
Başparmağımla, kelebek biçiminde
Çocukmuşum gibi aynanın önünde
Yüzümü saçlarımı okşuyorum

Kadıköy'den herhangi bir deniz
Tenha bir tramvay Şişliden
Samatya'dan belki Sultanahmet'ten
İncir ağaçları anımsıyorum

Göğsüme bir İstanbul çiziyorum
Başparmağımla, kelebek biçiminde
Biraz umutsuzum, biraz yorgun işte
En çok gözlerimi seviyorum

WHAT I LOST AMONG THE LILACS

Ah, those spring evenings so lovely
Joy on the far side of overwhelming realities
Horizons that daily recede like memories
The unsensed odor of lilacs all about me

The nights I madly played the mandolin
And you, my fairy of a child's fable
Love of my earliest dreams, unforgettable
That washed-clean, purified reflection

After the Ramadan cannons, the whistle I blew
In streets deserted and desolate
Ah, loneliness, beloved and great
Where are you?

I've lost among the lilacs a thing
Beautiful as never-lived remembrances
That cost me all joys, all brilliances
No, not even among the gods lingering

LEYLAKLARDA YİTİRDİĞİM

Ah o güzelim bahar akşamları
Kahredici gerçekler ötesinde kalan mutluluk
Günbegün anılarca uzaklaşan ufuk
Yöremde duyulmayan leylak kokuları

Delicesine mandolin çaldığım geceler
Ve sen, çocuk masallarımın perisi
İlk düşlerimin unutulmaz sevgilisi
O yunmuş, o arınmış düşünceler

Toplar atıldıktan sonra, kimsesiz
Terkedilmiş sokaklarda çaldığım ıslık
Ah o büyük, o dost yalnızlık
Nerelerdesiniz?

Bir şey var yitirdiğim leylaklarda
Yaşanmamış anılar kadar güzel
Tüm mutluluklara, aydınlıklara bedel
Hayır değil, değil tanrılarda

HARMONICA

I'm nuts about the whistle-blowing trains
In little stations, nights when it snows
Women smiling behind tulle curtains
I cling and pull myself up on the windows

I write a poem then sing a song
I sit there then and weep
Then do I blossom splendidly
Playing the harmonica in the street

Every night it rains in this city
And anew each night I'm dead and gone
Don't hide it, the train goes there
Say what you will, I'm getting on

MIZIKA

Karlı gecelerde küçük istasyonlarda
Düdük çalan trenlere bayılıyorum
Tül perdeler ardında kadınlar gülüyor
Tutup pencerelere tırmanıyorum

Bir şiir söylüyorum sonra bir şarkı
Sonra oturup ağlıyorum
Sonra bir güzel çiçeklenip
Sokaklarda mızıka çalıyorum

Bu şehre her gece yağmur yağıyor
Ve ben her gece yeniden ölüyorum
Bu tren oraya gidecek, gizlemeyin
Ne derseniz deyin ben biniyorum

AUTUMN MELODY

Lycée girls were crossing the avenue
The book of civil law I gently closed tight
It was about an exam, money, a label
I lit a cigarette out of spite.

For example, I said, this world
Spins and spins in a void
This rain, this beastly September rain
Drives a fellow completely insane
Okay, but people, people
What notion do they serve?

I thought, and thought touched me to the heart

Seconds, moments, hours, and soon
The days flow like water, my brother
On one hand the textbook, my heart on the other
I didn't know what to do

SONBAHAR EZGİSİ

Caddeden liseli kızlar geçiyordu
Medeni Hukuku usulca kapattım
İmtihanmış paraymış etiketmiş
İnadına bir sigara yaktım

Örneğin dedim şu dünya
Bir boşlukta döner de döner
Şu yağmur şu hınzır eylül yağmuru
Adamı büsbütün deli eder
Peki insanlar peki insanlar
Hangi akla hizmet eder

Düşünüp düşünüp içlendim

Saniyeler dakikalar saatler derken
Günler su gibi akıyor kardeşim
Bir yanda ders kitapları bir yanda kalbim
Şaşırdım kaldım

HOW AWFUL WHEN POETRY AGES AS IT IS READ

Three dots: And there was a city behind the blue curtains
Which Saturday, this the how-manyth pack, men would come
    from the bazaars
I was going to think up a street with sailboats, poppies in white caps
Some guy would drop his cigarette into the water
Gulls into the water, women proudly into the bazaars
I was going to write a poem, I was stifling, fed up with old things
Eat, my mother says, but they're all things I've grown accustomed to,
    in the end.
Like Camus and—I don't know—people like that, I'm cracking up
Everything will begin when it untangles itself from your hair

Is the truth of tablecloths to be spread? How awful always
    to take refuge in known words
A person should let himself go. —But what kind of color is this—
Evenings come, as though contemplating poetry, from a place
    close to inspiration
Quinces sweet and soft . . .
Later exaggerating the ache in my belly, I would be frightened
At that tubercular child's how-manyth deception they will come
Everything spills into a colorless void
Writing poems is perhaps the loveliest deception
Later they'll make a picture or something, then go and drink wine

OKUNDUKÇA NE KÖTÜ ESKİMESİ ŞİİRİN

Üç nokta; Ve mavi perdelerin ardında kent vardı
Hangi cumartesi, bu kaçıncı paket, adamlar gelirdi çarşılardan
Yelkenli bir sokak düşünecektim, beyaz şapkalı gelincikler
Adamın biri sigarasını suya düşürecekti
Martılar sulara, kadınlar gururla çarşılara
Ben şiir yazacaktım, canım sıkılıyordu, eski şeylerden bıkmıştım
Yemek ye, diyor annem, hep alışkanlıklarım sonunda
Kamü'ymüş, yok bilmem kimmiş, bilincim çatlayacak
Her şey senin saçlarından çözüldükten sonra başlayacak

Masa örtülerinin serilmek midir gerçeği? Hep bildik sözcük-
    lere sığınmak ne kötü
Koyvermeli kendini kişi. —Ama nasıl renk bu—
Esinçlerin yanında bir yerden akşamların şiir düşünür gibi-
    gelmesi
Tatlı ve yumuşak ayvalar . . .
Sonra midemin ağrıdığını büyütüp, korkacaktım
O veremli çocuğun kaçıncı aldanışında gelecekler
Her şey renksiz bir boşluğa dökülür
Şiir yazmak belki en güzel aldanıştır
Sonra resim filan yapacaklar, gidip şarap içecekler

I'd make me into a brand new sailor if I were God
Maybe there were new things over there
It comes from within me to write as though rabid, I'm hungry, do
    you understand
Let the doctors call it what they will
Who can know anything best of all
What does it mean to know anything best
Which religion doesn't grow old

My hands and my wrists and my eyes are tingling with desire
I don't ever want to see your wearied faces again
Within me is a dynamite of boredom and I'll die if it doesn't explode
I want to write poetry, I'm bored, disgusted by my habits
If I stop thinking and put my hands down perhaps I will have much to say
I'm scurrying to the attic like a solitary bug
Before you become old and ugly, I must kiss you on the nose

Kendimi yepyeni bir gemici yapardım Allah olsam
Ötelerde belki yeni şeyler vardı
Kudurmuş gibi yazmak geliyor içimden, açım anlıyor musun
Doktorlar buna ne derslerse desin
Kim en iyi bilebilir herhangi bir şeyi
Bir şeyi en iyi bilmek ne demektir
Hangi din eskimez

Ellerim ve bileklerim ve gözlerim şehvetle gıcıklanıyorlar
Yorgun suratlarınızı hiç mi hiç göresim gelmedi
İçimde bir sıkıntı dinamiti var ki patlamasa öleceğim
Şiir yazmak istiyorum, canım sıkılıyor, alışkanlıklarımdan iğreniyorum
Düşünmesem ve koyversem ellerimi belki çok şeyler söylerim
Tenha bir böcek gibi tavan arasına koşuyorum
Sen çirkin bir ihtiyar olmadan burnundan öpmeliyim

BLACK SONG

Once more in that hour of darkness
In dark black waters they arise
Dark songs pass before their eyes
They lie awake gazing into darkness

The woman's dark black hair
The man's hands dark black
Like whys without an answer back
The room, four sides, four black walls

A line with two ends in darkness
In the darkness they were deceived
Dark verses in darkness they conceived
And like two blacks were silent

In the most affirming places of their love
Suddenly they grew tired, out of breath
Little by little they felt the death
Of some places left in darkness

KARA ŞARKI

Karanlığın yine o saatinde
Kapkara sularda uyandılar
Gözlerinden karanlık şarkılar geçiyordu
Uzanıp karanlığa baktılar

Kadının kapkara saçları
Kapkara elleri adamın
Yanıtsız sorular gibi-odanın
Dört yanında dört kara duvar

İki ucu karanlıkta bir çizginin
Karanlık ortasında aldandılar
Kapkara mısralar kurdular karanlıkta
Ve iki zenci gibi sustular

En olumlu yerinde sevgilerinin
Birden soluk soluğa yoruldular
Azar azar öldüğünü duydular
Karanlıkta kalan bir yerlerinin

CAT

"Farewell, farewell" how nice is that
A third one leaves the harmony flat
"Farewell, farewell, farewell"
What's more, it seems just like a cat

The fellow's head is mighty large
In his pocket a novel of Sartre's
Looking neither left nor right
Perhaps for heaven he departs

Ataol abhors it when it rains
Don't ask the time, he's scared to tell
Every time I sit down for a raki
Here comes the third "farewell"

KEDİ

"Elveda, elveda" ne güzel.
Üçüncü, uyumu bozuyor.
"Elveda, elveda, elveda"
Üstelik kediye benziyor.

Adamın kafası kocaman
Cebinde Sartre'dan bir roman
Sağına soluna bakmadan
Belki de cennete gidiyor

Ataol yağmuru sevmiyor
Saati sormayın korkuyor
Ne zaman rakıya otursam
Üçüncü elveda geliyor

OH, FAR OFF

Illumined were my most ancient sorrows
Increasing, amid all rules, my primordial longing
What was lived in my stream of love, who knows
Which ships were they, over dark seas passing

She filled her basket with lilac blossoms
His joy exceeded all familiar bounds
A fair-haired man, woman with pink teeth
Birds alone know how their secret kisses sound

Was it in the sudden silence, like the rivers
In the dark of night meaningful and weighty
To die by thousands, from a thousand places, years
For a thousand years, to grow toward you and eternity

Who was it in the caverns' warm gloaming
The tiny friendly kisses, so like my mother's
Telling of love, gently hinting at something other
Gently into the forest of feeling roaming

May it never end, please, let it endure in silence
Which knows how to weep, nostalgic and masculine
Which falls like snow quietly into my eyes
Now just to worship you, oh, far off violin

EY UZAK

O en eski hüznümdür benim aydınlanan
Kurallar boyu büyüten ilkel özlemimi
Kim bilir sevgi ırmağımda nelerdi yaşanan
Karanlık denizlerden geçen hangi gemilerdi

Sepetine eflatun çiçekler doldurmuş
Mutluluğu bildik biçimlere sığmayan
Sarışın bir adam, pembe dişli bir kadın
Kuşlardır en gizli öpüşlerini duyan

Ansızın susuşunda mı, nehirler gibi
Ağır ve anlamlı, gecenin ortasında
Binlerce yerden binlerce ölmek bin yıl
Bin yıl büyümek sana ve sonsuza

Kimdi o, sıcak loşluğunda mağaraların
Dost öpücükleri anneme benzeyen
Sevgi anlatan, bir şeyler sezdiren usulca
Usulca alıp başını duygunun ormanına giden

Bitmesin, bitmesin ne olur bu sessiz uzayan
Bu kar yağar gibi usuldan gözlerime
Erkek ve özlemli ve ağlamasını bilen
Şimdi bir sana tapınmak ey uzak keman

SABIHA

Gimme a cigarette, my mother died
She died this morning around five I suppose
Allah Allah, my dear, what's the big surprise
I told you, that's all, my mother died

Don't look at me like that, you'll make me laugh
If we had a mirror, you'd see how dumb you look
Just my touch would make you too laugh
Why don't you give up playing it by the book

This past year she didn't even play the violin
As her wrinkles multiplied, she grew angry
Blaming Dad, as if they were his fault
And she kept on saying, no one understands me

If you want, let's go to the movies or something
There's a Nadia film playing at the Tayyareh
My younger brother cried a lot yesterday evening
Really, what's up with Sabiha anyway?

SABİHA

Bana bir sigara verin annem öldü
Bu sabah öldü beşe doğru sanırım
Allah Allah ne var şaşıracak canım
Annem öldü diyorum hepsi bu

Yüzüme bakmayın öyle gülesim geliyor
Bir ayna olsa da aptallığınızı görseniz
Hani dokunsam siz de güleceksiniz
Boş verin kurallara murallara yahu

Şu son yıl keman bile çalmadı
Yüzünde çizgiler çoğaldıkça öfkelendi
Sanki suçlu oymuş gibi babama yüklendi
Beni kimse anlayamaz deyip durdu

İsterseniz sinemaya falan gidelim
Galiba Nadya'nın bir filmi var Tayyare'de
Ortanca birader çok ağladı dün gece
Sahi, Sabiha işi ne oldu?

A VERY STRANGE BLACK

There, where Walt Whitman is from, a black
In Harlem, its leaves after rain
A glass of gin, double martini
As if feeling my self there in the dark

In Harlem, its leaves after rain
My hands and flesh that I left behind
If I don't shut up, I'll lose my mind
It's like I have another me in train

A glass of gin, double martini
I thought of your loveliest places
I thought of your loveliest places in the ugliest places
To forget and to die involved so little pain

As if feeling my self there in the dark
I perceived so many strange things
On Harlem a strange rain had begun to fall
There, where Walt Whitman is from, three blacks

ÇOK GARİP BİR ZENCİ

Walt Whitman'ın oralardan bir zenci
Harlem'de yağmur sonu yaprakları
Bir kadeh cin bir duble cin vermut
Karanlıkta ben'i duyar gibi

Harlem'de yağmur sonu yaprakları
Bırakılmış ellerim, etim
Susmasam kendi sesimden delirecektim
Benimle sanki bir başka ben vardı

Bir kadeh cin bir duble cin vermut
Sizin en güzel yerlerinizi düşündüm
En güzel yerlerinizi en çirkin yerde düşündüm
Unutmak ve ölmek o kadar kolaydı

Karanlıkta ben'i duyar gibi
Çok garip bir şeyler seziyordum
Harlem'e çok garip bir yağmur başlamıştı
Walt Whitman'ın oralardan üç zenci

THIS LOVE ENDS HERE

This love ends here and me . . . I'm up and gone
Child in my heart, in my pocket a revolver
This love ends here, have a good day, lover
And me, I'm up and gone, a river flowing on

It's a memory now, the city dozing heedless
While in albums children and soldiers yellow
Your face fades away like a wildflower
Bit by bit they deepen, sleep and forgetfulness

Side by side we lay and the grass was moist
How lovely you were, the summer without peer
Ever have they told of this; that is, of love lost
All the dead poets, as they passed from this sphere

This love ends here and me . . . I'm up and gone
Child in my heart, in my pocket a revolver
This love ends here, have a good day, lover
And me, I'm up and gone, a river flowing on

BU AŞK BURADA BİTER

Bu aşk burada biter ve ben çekip giderim
Yüreğimde bir çocuk cebimde bir revolver
Bu aşk burada biter iyi günler sevgilim
Ve ben çekip giderim bir nehir akıp gider

Bir hatıradır şimdi dalgın uyuyan şehir
Solarken albümlerde çocuklar ve askerler
Yüzün bir kır çiçeği gibi usulca söner
Uyku ve unutkanlık gittikçe derinleşir

Yan yana uzanırdık ve ıslaktı çimenler
Ne kadar güzeldin sen! nasıl eşsiz bir yazdı!
Bunu anlattılar hep, yani yiten bir aşkı
Geçerek bu dünyadan bütün ölü şairler

Bu aşk burada biter ve ben çekip giderim
Yüreğimde bir çocuk cebimde bir revolver
Bu aşk burada biter iyi günler sevgilim
Ve ben çekip giderim bir nehir akıp gider

II ONE DAY SURELY

ONE DAY SURELY

Today I made love and then I joined in a march
I'm exhausted, it's spring, I've got to learn to shoot a gun this summer
The books pile up, my hair's getting long, everywhere there's a
   rumble of anxiety
I'm still young, I want to see the world, how lovely it is
   to kiss, how lovely to think, one day surely we'll win
One day surely we'll win, you money changers of old,
   you goose brains, you grand vizier!
My beloved is an eighteen-year-old girl, we're walking down
   the avenue, eating a sandwich, talking about the world
Flowers blossom ceaselessly, the wars go on, how can everything end
   with a bomb, how can they win, those filthy men
Long I ponder, I wash my face over and over, dress myself
   in a clean shirt
This tyranny will end one day, this feast of plunder will end
But I'm tired now, I'm smoking a lot, a dirty overcoat on my back
Furnace smoke rises into the sky, in my pockets
   books of poetry in Vietnamese
I think of my friends at the other ends of the earth,
   of the rivers at its other ends
A girl dies quietly, dies quietly over there
I'm crossing bridges, on a dark and rainy day, walking
   to the station
These houses are making me sad, this slapdash world
People, the sounds of motors, fog, the water flowing on
What to do . . . what to do . . . everywhere the dregs of sadness
I lean my brow against cool iron, those old days come to mind
And me . . . I was a child, I would surely have things to love
I'm thinking about coming back from the movies, about my mother,
   how can everything die, how can someone be forgotten

BİR GÜN MUTLAKA

Bugün seviştim, yürüyüşe katıldım sonra
Yorgunum, bahar geldi, silah kullanmayı öğrenmeliyim bu yaz
Kitaplar birikiyor, saçlarım uzuyor, her yerde gümbür
    gümbür bir telâş
Gencim daha, dünyayı görmek istiyorum, öpüşmek ne
    güzel, düşünmek ne güzel, bir gün mutlaka yeneceğiz!
Bir gün mutlaka yeneceğiz, ey eski zaman sarrafları! Ey kaz
    kafalılar! Ey sadrazam!
Sevgilim on sekizinde bir kız, yürüyoruz bulvarda, sandviç
    yiyoruz, dünyadan konuşuyoruz.
Çiçekler açıyor durmadan, savaşlar oluyor, her şey nasıl
    bitebilir bir bombayla, nasıl kazanabilir o kirli adamlar
Uzun uzun düşünüyor, sularla yıkıyorum yüzümü temiz
    bir gömlek giyiyorum
Bitecek bir gün bu zulüm, bitecek bu hân-ı yağma
Ama yorgunum, şimdi, çok sigara içiyorum, sırtımda kirli bir pardesü
Kalorifer dumanları çıkıyor göğe, cebimde Vietnamca şiir
    kitapları
Dünyanın öbür ucundaki dostları düşünüyorum öbür
    ucundaki ırmakları
Bir kız sessizce ölüyor, sessizce ölüyor orda
Köprülerden geçiyorum, karanlık yağmurlu bir gün, yürü-
    yorum istasyona
Bu evler hüzünlendiriyor beni, bu derme çatma dünya
İnsanlar, motor sesleri, sis, akıp giden su
Ne yapsam . . . ne yapsam . . . her yerde bir hüzün tortusu
Alnımı soğuk bir demire dayıyorum, o eski günler geliyor aklıma
Ben de çocuktum, sevgilerim olacaktı elbette
Sinema dönüşlerini düşünüyorum, annemi, her şey nasıl
    ölebilir, nasıl unutulur insan

Oh sky! I used to lie still beneath you, oh you gleaming fields
What to do . . . What to do . . . later I was reading Descartes . . .
My beard's getting long, I'm in love with this girl, it's just
    a little hike to Chankaya
A Sunday, a sun-lit Sunday, how tumultuous is my heart,
    how I mingle with the people
A child peers from a window, a child with great dreamy eyes
Then his brother looks out, who resembles the childhood
    portraits of Lermontov
I'm writing a poem at the typewriter, I'm intrigued by the
    newspapers, the sounds of birds come to my ears
I'm a modest poet, my beloved, everything gets me excited
So what is there to cry about, when gazing on the common man
I'm looking at the guy's ears, his neck, his eyes,
    eyebrows, the play of his face
Oh people, I say, oh child, and as I say it I feel like crying
I curse all the individualist poets, I'm going to the market
    to buy an orange
I curse those chattering crowds, their withered hearts,
    the liberation of the individual and the like
I curse those bookworms, and then I forgive them all
After long winter nights, who knows how things happen
After long winter nights that are told of in legends
Over and over I think on these things, a joy follows
    close upon a sorrow
My heart is a changeable springtime sky, in short, a Turkish heart
Waiting's left me fed up, I'm anxiously explaining things left and right
I get on a bus, I'm intently inspecting a bug held by
    the wings
I used to walk in the spring to the fields
    where those ruins and pastures are

Ey gök! senin altında sessizce yatardım, ey pırıl pırıl tarlalar
Ne yapsam . . . ne yapsam . . . Dekart okuyorum sonradan . . .
Sakallarım uzuyor, ben bu kızı seviyorum, ufak bir yürüyüş
    Çankaya'ya
Bir pazar, güneşli bir pazar, nasıl coşuyor yüreğim, nasıl
    karışıyorum insanlara
Bir çocuk bakıyor pencereden, hülyalı kocaman gözlü nefis bir çocuk
Lermontov'un çocukluk fotoğraflarına benzeyen kardeşi
    bakıyor sonra
Ben şiir yazıyorum daktiloda, gazeteleri merak ediyorum,
    kuş sesleri geliyor kulağıma
Ben mütevazı bir şairim, sevgilim, her şey coşkulandırıyor beni
Sanki ağlayacak ne var bakarken bir halk adamına
Bakıyorum adamın kulaklarına, boynuna, gözlerine, kaşla-
    rına, yüzünün oynamasına
Ey halk diyorum, ey çocuk, derken bende bir ağlama
İlençliyorum bütün bireyci şairleri, hale gidiyorum portakal
    almaya
İlençliyorum o laf kalabalıklarını, kurumuş yürekleri,
    bireyin kurtuluşunu filan
İlençliyorum o kitap kurtlarını, bağışlıyorum sonradan
Uzun kış gecelerinden sonra, kim bilir nasıl olur her şey
Uzun kış gecelerinden sonra, masallarda anlatılan
Durup durup bunları düşünüyorum, bir sevinci bir hüzün
    izliyor arkadan
Yüreğim ipesapa gelmez bir bahar göğü, Türkçe bir yürek kısaca
Beklemek usandırıyor, telaşlı telaşlı bir şeyler anlatıyorum sağda solda
Bir otobüse biniyorum, inceliyorum bir böceği tutarak
    kanatlarından merakla
Yürürdüm eskiden baharda, o yıkıntıların ve çayırların
    olduğu alanlara

One day surely we'll defeat you, one day surely we'll defeat
      you, we'll say it a thousand times
Then a thousand times more, then a thousand times more, we'll
      multiply it with marching songs
I and my beloved and my friends, we will all march down the boulevard
We will march with the enthusiasm of being created anew
Ever multiplying we will march . . .

Bir gün mutlaka yeneceğiz! Bir gün mutlaka yeneceğiz!
Bunu söyleyeceğiz bin defa!
Sonra bin defa daha, sonra bin defa daha, çoğaltacağız
marşlarla
Ben ve sevgilim ve arkadaşlar yürüyeceğiz bulvarda
Yürüyeceğiz yeniden yaratılmanın coşkusuyla
Yürüyeceğiz çoğala çoğala . . .

WHEN LEAVING TOWN

The things recalled when leaving town
Are mostly little things
The grocer's bill is paid
At the last moment, one runs into a distant acquaintance

What is a town and what is it
That a town leaves to a person
Dusty roads stretching on and on
End up with flat mountains

When leaving town, it's a familiar thing
To leave a woman behind too
You would walk into the groves
Carrying her face with you

And always in the flowing of streams
Something that reminded you of the past
Was it because they were turbid
Or did summer quietly grow old at last

Summers, towns, and women
The acrid taste of leaving love behind you
Something all children
And all poets are living through

BİR KENTİ BIRAKIRKEN ANIMSANAN

Bir kenti bırakırken anımsanan
Daha çok küçük şeylerdir
Bakkalın borcu ödenir
Ve uzak bir tanıdığa rastlanır son anda

Bir kent nedir ve bir insana
Bıraktığı şey nedir bir kentin
Uzayıp giden tozlu yollar
Sonuçlanır yassı dağlarla

Bir kenti bırakırken, alışılmış
Bir şeydir bırakmak bir kadını da
Yürürdün koruluklara
Yüzünü taşıyarak onun

Ve çayların akışında her zaman
Eskiyi anımsatan bir şey vardı
Bulanık olduklarından mı
Yoksa yaz mı eskirdi usulca

Yazlar kentler ve kadınlar
Bir aşkı bırakmanın buruk tadı
Bütün çocukların ve bütün
Şairlerin hep yaşadığı

POEM ON A CHILD'S DREAM

In a child's dream always
There is a lost beloved
The rag and bone man stole her
Unexpectedly toward evening

The coolness of the fields comes
Lights on the forehead of a child
And so, while they sleep, the foreheads
Of children are white and taut

Your childhood too is a relative
Of summer gardens and apples
The dust has risen of a late afternoon
From the slope over by the graveyard

A lost love always
Resembles a lost marble
Its glitter recalled
In barely visible tears

In a child's dream at times
A vanished marble is found
The cherry trees sway
Pigeons rise in a flock to the sky

BİR ÇOCUĞUN RÜYASI İÇİN ŞİİR

Bir çocuğun rüyasında her zaman
Kaybolmuş bir sevgili vardır
Onu eskiciler çalmıştır
Bir akşamüstü hiç umulmadan

Kırların serinliği gelir
Konar bir çocuğun alnına
Onun için uyurken alınları
Beyaz ve gergindir çocukların

Senin de çocukluğun akrabadır
Yaz bahçeleriyle elmalarla
Tozlar kalkmıştır bir akşamüstü
Mezarlığın ordaki bayırdan

Kaybolmuş bir sevgi her zaman
Kaybolmuş bir bilyaya benzer
Anımsanır ışıltısı
Belli belirsiz gözyaşlarıyla

Bir çocuğun rüyasında bazen
Bulunur kaybolmuş bir bilya
Kiraz ağaçları sallanır
Güvercinler uçuşur havada

ENGLAND:

WITH DYLAN THOMAS

Above the Thames
On a suspension bridge
As September ran
Its fingers
Through my hair;
It were no surprise
If I had met up
With Dylan Thomas.

IN LONDON

I could have died
Of grief in London
If grief
Did not suit this city so

İNGİLTERE:

DYLAN THOMAS'LA

Thames üstünde
Bir asma köprüde
Eylül gezdiriyorken
Parmaklarını
Saçlarımda;
Şaşırmazdım
Karşılaşsaydık
Dylan Thomas'la

LONDRA'DA

Kederden
Ölebilirdim Londra'da
Keder
Bu kente yakışmasa

SONNET

In Paris the houses seem polished bright
Especially on late sun-lit afternoons
Sprawled on its warm courtyard stones
Paris is a woman, languorous and white

Then the first stirrings, the first people
And this will turn to an evening reverie
Paris . . . weird, confusing, enigma city
Paris . . . sightless, heartless, and brutal

The Eiffel Tower on its great dragon frame
Bears a miniscule fist-sized brain
Witless, dull-eyed, now grows near now distant

Collapse there, if you will, for love or lack of hope
If you will, scream there, go mad, or just croak
This town will exceed you at every instant

SONNET

Paris'te evler cilalanmış gibidir
Özellikle güneşli öğle sonlarında
Paris, ısınmış taşlıklarına
Baygın, beyaz bir kadın gibi serilir . . .

Sonra ilk kıpırtılar, ilk insanlar
Ve bu, bir akşam rüyasına dönüşecektir . . .
Paris, tuhaf, çapraşık, anlaşılmaz şehir,
Paris, kör, kalpsiz, canavar . . .

Ve Eiffel, ejderha gövdesinin üstünde
Yumruk kadar ufak bir beyin taşır . . .
Bön, sersem gözleriyle yaklaşıp uzaklaşır . . .

İstersen yıkıl oraya, aşktan, ümitsizlikten;
Bağır, çıldır, geber istersen . . .
Bu şehir seni her an aşacaktır . . .

WHO, ME? OKAY . . .

Who, me? Okay . . .
One day I'm out of here, leaving behind the doors,
        the houses, the journals, and the woes
A flower will say, "Hi there"
A mountain will say, "Welcome"
A forest will smile
In the place where recollections, expectations, hope, and hopelessness
Where greed, competitions, worries depart
In the place where narration alone, pure narration,
        remains, there poetry will begin . . .
Which speaks to no one, sufficient only unto itself
Coherent within its own logic, its own beauty
But the life of the people will enter therein, because
        the people are a living thing, a mighty thing
And the sea and horizon will enter, anthills, sky, and pinecones
And sea foam and, in the end, a love without jealousy
I mean, to make love with the sea, unconditionally,
        without prejudice or reckoning
I mean, to lie down and think for thousands of years
Of things that are born, and die, and live on
Of being born, of dying, and of living
To tell of everything dormant and great
Me? Okay. One day I'm out of here . . .
Without worries or tears, leaving nothing behind,
        expecting nothing ahead
Nothing but a sparkling clean heart made of rainwater
With a heart that, in the end, has only its own meaning,
        its own reasons.

BEN Mİ? EVET...

Ben mi? Evet...
Bir gün çıkıp gideceğim kapıları evleri dergileri hüzünleri
    bırakarak...
Bir çiçek merhaba diyecek...
Hoş geldin diyecek dağ...
Orman gülümseyecek...
Anımsayışların, bekleyişlerin, ümitlerin ya da ümitsizliklerin
Hırsların, yarışların, tasaların kalktığı yerde
Tam anlatının, salt anlatının kaldığı yerde başlayacak şiir...
Hiç kimseye seslenmeyen, kendi kendine yeten sadece...
Kendi mantığı, kendi güzelliği içinde tutarlı...
Ama halkın yaşantısı girecektir oraya, çünkü yaşayan, büyük
    bir şeydir halk...
Deniz ve ufuk girecek, karınca yuvaları, gökyüzü, kozalaklar
Ve köpük ve artık hasetsiz bir aşk...
Yani sevişmek denizle, koşulsuz, önyargısız, hesapsız...
Yani uzanmak ve düşünmek binlerce yıl...
Doğan, ölen ve yaşayan şeyleri...
Doğumu, ölümü ve yaşamayı.
Yani dingin ve büyük olan her şeyi anlatmak.
Ben mi? Evet. Çıkıp gideceğim bir gün...
Tasasız, gözyaşsız, geride bir şey bırakmadan ve bir şey
    beklemeden ilerde...
Sadece yağmur sularından pırıl pırıl bir yürek
Artık kendi kendinin anlamı ve nedeni olan bir yürekle...

ONE MORNING WHILE ENTERING A FAMILIAR CITY

One morning, while entering a familiar city,
A fellow thinks of things warm and friendly
A familiar bed awaits you
A child's face smiles out of the memory

Friendly cities, beloved, mother cities
How many sorrows and joys I lived in each of you
With a young man's wild bliss, I walked your streets
I had days of mind-wrenching grief too

Like a film with an infinity of frames
My life passes through my memory
The feeling of repeating
Everything, anew and anew

One morning, while entering a familiar city,
A fellow thinks of things melancholy and strange
Because he senses that not only the city
But he himself has changed

BİR SABAH TANIDIK BİR ŞEHRE GİRERKEN

Bir sabah tanıdık bir şehre girerken
Sıcak ve dost şeyler düşünür insan
Tanıdık bir yatak bekler sizi
Bir çocuk yüzü gülümser anılardan

Dost şehirler, sevgili, anne şehirler
Nice acılar, nice mutluluklar yaşadım her birinizde
Delikanlı bir sevinçle sokaklarınızdan geçtiğim oldu
Kederli günlerim oldu aklımı yitiresiye

Sonsuz kareli bir film gibi
Yaşamım geçiyor belleğimden
Tekrar etmek duygusu
Her şeyi yeniden yeniden

Bir sabah tanıdık bir şehre girerken
Kederli, tuhaf şeyler düşünür insan
Sadece o şehrin değil
Kendisinin de değiştiği duygusundan . . .

WHAT DO THE GREEK SONGS SAY

What do the Greek songs say
About nighttime, about love
What do the Greek songs say
About how we live

What do the Greek songs say
With this melancholy that wraps a person head to toe
It is as if an unsaid something always remains
However much we reveal what is inside of us

What do the Greek songs say
Is it the end of a love, or a love beginning
Is it a girl, whose face we will never see
Countryside in whose meadows we can never lie

What do the Greek songs say
With this continuous, this soft insistence
What do the Greek songs say
With rhythms that seep into our hearts

What do the Greek songs say
About eternal beauty, peace eternally;
No matter how much we fill them with pain
They're about living oh so ardently

What do the Greek songs say
Is it that all songs will one day be one
What do the Greek songs say
So distant . . . yet not so far away

NE ANLATIR YUNAN ŞARKILARI

Ne anlatır Yunan şarkıları
Geceye dair, aşka dair
Ne anlatır Yunan şarkıları
Hayatımıza dair

Ne anlatır Yunan şarkıları
İnsanı tepeden tırnağa saran bu hüzünle
Sanki hep anlatılmayan bir şey kalmıştır
İçimizi ne kadar döksek de

Ne anlatır Yunan şarkıları
Biten bir aşk mı, başlayan bir aşk mı
Bir kız mı, yüzünü hiç görmeyeceğimiz
Çayırlarına hiç uzanamayacağımız kırlar mı

Ne anlatır Yunan şarkıları
Bu sürekli, bu yumuşak ısrarla
Ne anlatır Yunan şarkıları
Yüreğimize işleyen tempolarla

Ne anlatır Yunan şarkıları
Sonsuz güzelliğe, sonsuz barışa dair
Acılarla dolsak da ne kadar
Sımsıcak yaşamaya dair

Ne anlatır Yunan şarkıları
Bir gün birleşeceğini mi bütün şarkıların
Ne anlatır Yunan şarkıları
Bu kadar uzak . . . ve bu kadar yakın

BESIEGED

Under siege I am obliged to make
Decisions that will shape my doom
Not in secluded gardens
Do I live love, but in flimsy rooms

As soon as I find the loveliest line
The sound of a car horn disrupts my reveries
In my mind thoughts about my life
On my pants a spot of grease

A smirking, importunate ad spot
Tacked onto an emotional movie
Love is losing its meaning
And vengefulness growing slippery

Side by side with a child's corpse
A laughing child lives within
How to feel unadulterated joy
And how to sorrow . . . both we have forgotten

Once there was a thing called sky
Endless, vast, and blue
Now, ratty clouds like sickly hounds
Are skulking aimlessly around

And the sea enchained by breakwaters
Bit by bit becomes a stagnant pool
Letting flow its poison into nature
Is the swamp within us all

KUŞATMADA

Kuşatma altında vermem gerekiyor
Ömrümü etkileyecek kararları.
Kuytu bahçelerde değil
Sarsak odalarda yaşıyorum aşkı.

En güzel dizeyi buluyorum derken
Bozuyor düşümü bir klakson sesi
Aklımda hayatım üstüne düşünceler
Ve pantolonumdaki yağ lekesi.

Sırıtkan, sırnaşık bir reklam spotu
Ekleniyor sonuna duygulu bir filmin
Sevgi yitiriyor anlamını
Kaypaklaşıyor kin.

Bir çocuk ölüsüyle yan yana
Yaşıyor içimde gülen çocuk.
Katıksız sevinç duymayı
Ve üzülmeyi artık unuttuk.

Gök diye bir şey vardı bir zaman
Sonsuz, engin, mavi
Şimdi sünepe bulutların
Hasta köpekler gibi gezindiği

Ve dalgakıranlarla zincirlenmiş deniz
Gitgide çürüyen bir su olmada artık
Akıtmada zehrini doğaya
İçimizdeki bataklık ...

Under siege I am obliged to make
Decisions that will shape my doom
But nothing can dry up the love
That green in arid soil, I make bloom

Kuşatma altında vermem gerekiyor
Ömrümü etkileyecek kararları,
Fakat hiçbir şey kurutamayacak
Çorak topraklarda yeşerttiğim aşkı . . .

III TURKEY, MY UNHAPPY LAND, MY LOVELY LAND

THROUGH THOSE POOR, UNLIT STREETS

While walking, toward evening, through those poor, unlit streets
Homeward, a net bag of groceries in my hand
Wiped away seems the weariness of my mind
I'm warmed inside by a sense of being the people's bard

Like a red rose in the worn hands
Of a flower seller in the street

ŞU YOKSUL, IŞIKSIZ SOKAKLARDAN

Şu yoksul, ışıksız sokaklardan geçerken akşamüstleri
Elimde yiyecek filesi, evime doğru
Siliniyor sanki zihnimin yorgunluğu
Isıtıyor halkımın ozanı olmak duygusu içimi

Yıpranmış ellerinde bir sokak çiçekçisinin
Bir kırmızı gül gibi

PREGNANT WOMAN'S SONG

Weather's chill, God damn it all
Detergent's cracked my hands so sore
As if three kids were not enough
This next one makes it four

Wash the risers, light the stove, and throw the trash away
Does the fault belong with me or that man of mine, what say?

Oh mama, he kicks me hard
He'll pierce my gut, I fear
Come on babe, do you suppose
It's all holidays out here?

To the grocer's, wash the clothes, and throw the trash away
Does the fault belong with me or that man of mine, what say?

Okay ma'am, I'm on my way
God willing, you'll go dumb
I've had it, Lord. It's snow 'n storm
On the peaks of Erzurum

Wash the dishes, cook the food, and throw the trash away
Does the fault belong with me or that man of mine, what say?

Weather's chill, God damn it all
Detergent's cracked my hands so sore
As if three kids were not enough
This next one makes it four

GEBE KADININ TÜRKÜSÜ

Hava da bi ayaz allahın cezası
Ellerim yarıldı deterjandan
Üç tane velet yetmezmiş gibi
Dördüncü geliyor ardından

Merdivenleri sil, kaloriferi yak, çöpü at
Kabahat benim mi, kocamın kabahat

Uy anam bi de tekmeliyo ki
Sanırsın karnımı delecek
Dışarıda bayram var seyran var bellersin
Bok mu var erken gelecek

Bakkala git, çamaşır yıka, çöpü at
Kabahat benim mi, kocamın kabahat

Tamam hanım geliyom tamam
Sesin kesilir inşallah
Erzurum dağları da kar ile boran
Canımdan usandım vallah

Bulaşığı yıka, yemeği pişir, çöpü at
Kabahat benim mi, kocamın kabahat

Hava da bi ayaz allahın cezası
Ellerim yarıldı deterjandan
Üç tane velet yetmezmiş gibi
Dördüncü geliyor ardından

Wash the risers, light the stove, and throw the trash away
Does the fault belong with me or that man of mine, what say?

Merdivenleri sil, kaloriferi yak, çöpü at
Kabahat benim mi, kocamın kabahat

THE POOR MAN'S MORNING SONG

Morning's the mother of beauty they said
But morning for us is not any such thing
Ours is a curse upon our heads

Once they heard the guitar's lament
Broken was morning's drinking bowl
But morning for us is not any such thing
First makes a baby hungry, then howl

They say the sleep of a morning's sweet
Never tasted it and never will
Morning is come, morning is come
Of sleep I never got my fill

In its bed the wind sleeps on
Rivers slumber in their beds
And I awake in the dark of morn
While the bosses sleep sound in their beds

Morning's the mother of beauty they said
But morning for us is not any such thing
Ours is a curse upon our heads

Once they heard the guitar's lament
Broken was morning's drinking bowl
But morning for us is not any such thing
First makes a baby hungry, then howl

YOKSULUN SABAH TÜRKÜSÜ

Sabah bütün güzelliklerin anasıdır
Bizim sabahımız öyle değil
Bizimki başımızın belasıdır

Gitarın ağlayışı duyuldu mu
Kırılırmış sabahın kadehi
Bizim sabahımız öyle değil
Önce acıktırır ağlatır bebeği

Tatlı olurmuş sabah uykusu
Ben tadını alamadım
Sabah oldu sabah oldu
Uykuya kanamadım

Rüzgâr uyur yatağında
Sular yatağında uyur
Uyanırım sabahın köründe
Beyler yatağında uyur

Sabah bütün güzelliklerin anasıdır
Bizim sabahımız öyle değil
Bizimki başımızın belasıdır

Gitarın ağlayışı duyuldu mu
Kırılırmış sabahın kadehi
Bizim sabahımız öyle değil
Önce acıktırır ağlatır bebeği

THE SONG OF TIME PASSING

The wheels they spin spin yes they spin
They spin yes they spin days of my youth

The belts they pass pass yes they pass
They pass yes they pass days of my youth

And time it flows flows yes it flows
They flow yes they flow days of my youth

The world it spins spins yes it spins
They spin yes they spin days of my youth

The days they pass pass yes they pass
They pass yes they pass days of my youth

The days they flow flow yes they flow
They flow yes they flow days of my youth

The wheels they spin spin yes they spin
They spin yes they spin days of my youth

The belts they pass pass yes they pass
They pass yes they pass days of my youth

And time it flows flows yes it flows
They flow yes they flow days of my youth

AKIP GİDEN ZAMAN TÜRKÜSÜ

Döner çarklar döner ha döner
Döner ha döner gençliğim

Geçer bantlar geçer ha geçer
Geçer ha geçer gençliğim

Akar zaman akar ha akar
Akar ha akar gençliğim

Döner dünya döner ha döner
Döner ha döner gençliğim

Geçer günler geçer ha geçer
Geçer ha geçer gençliğim

Akar günler akar ha akar
Akar ha akar gençliğim

Döner çarklar döner ha döner
Döner ha döner gençliğim

Geçer bantlar geçer ha geçer
Geçer ha geçer gençliğim

Akar zaman akar ha akar
Akar ha akar gençliğim

SCHOOLROOM ADVICE AND RESPONSE

—White silver is for blackest days
So save up your money well.
—And one who lacks for daily needs
What should he do teacher, pray tell?

—Our elders often said to us
Drop by drop one makes a lake.
—But about this lake, please teacher say
How long does the making take?

—He who can't do with little can never find a lot
So we should learn to get along with no more than a jot.
—Then you might have also said that one will surely find
In a body of diminished health, a less than healthy mind.

—A tree bends down when it is green
Get this proverb by heart just so.
—But it suits a man to be standing tall
You said just a moment ago.

—Happiness is the end of patience
For us to know patience is fine.
—But what if the rock of patience
One day cracks, oh teacher mine?

OKULDA ÖĞÜTLER VE YANITLAR

—Ak akçe kara gün içindir
Fazla paranızı biriktirin.
—Ya parası bugüne yetmeyen
Ne yapmalı öğretmenim?

—Damlaya damlaya göl olur
Demiş büyüklerimiz.
—Öğretmenim bu göl
Ne kadar sürede oluşur dersiniz?

—Aza kanaat etmeyen çoğu hiç bulamaz
Azla yetinmeyi bilmeliyiz.
—Öyleyse az sağlam vücutta
Az sağlam kafa bulunur demeliydiniz . . .

—Ağaç yaşken eğilir
Bu atasözünü ezberleyin.
—Ama insana dik durmak yaraşır
Diyordunuz demin . . .

—Sabrın sonu esenliktir
Yeter ki sabretmesini bilelim.
—Ya sabır taşı bir gün
Çatlarsa öğretmenim?

SONG TO SODAS

When the world grows dim in your eyes
And things seem one hell of a mess
Just have a few sodas
Yes, this is happiness

Your child's rickety, coughs himself hoarse
Your husband's exhausted each day
Just have a few sodas
And get down to merriment's source

Everything goes easier
With a few sodas
Loves appear greenly
And sprout up with sodas

Sodas in the home, sodas in the market
And sodas, you see, even at school
Just have a few sodas
And cast off worries from your soul

When the world grows dim in your eyes
And things seem one hell of a mess
Just have a few sodas
Yes, this is happiness

MEŞRUBAT TÜRKÜSÜ

Dünya gözünde karardı mı
Her şey içinden çıkılmaz oldu mu
Meşrubat iç
İşte mutluluk bu

Çocuğun sıska, öksürüklü
Kocan gün günden yorgun
Meşrubat iç
İn kaynağına mutluluğun

Meşrubatla her şey
Daha iyi gider
Yeşerir, boy atar
Meşrubatla sevgiler

Evde meşrubat, pazarda meşrubat
İşte, okulda meşrubat
Meşrubat iç
Tasayı gönlünden at

Dünya gözünde karardı mı
Her şey içinden çıkılmaz oldu mu
Meşrubat iç
İşte mutluluk bu

(From) LETTERS TO MY DAUGHTER
(In Secret)

1.
My little girl, my little girl, my little girl
You were all sparkles when I saw you last
You were happy, you were trusting

Yet it was the last time I came to see you
Before we were parted.

How could you have known you'd be orphaned
Even at that moment, how.

I kissed your face, your eyes
Then, like a fugitive, departed
Our house, our neighborhood

A harsh wind beats now on the lowered
Shutters of the room where I stay
In your little heart, ill-defined anxiety
Perhaps, you are thinking too of me.

Before us, a long separation
Lasting months and maybe years.
I will either look upon you next
From behind the chain links
Without kissing, smelling
Your face, your hands
Or from afar, in exile
Make do with your voice alone.

"KIZIMA MEKTUPLAR"dan
(Gizlilikte)

1.
Küçük kızım küçük kızım küçük kızım
Işıl ışıldın son gördüğümde
Mutluydun, güvenliydin

Oysa seni son kez görmeye gelişimdi
Ayrılık öncesinde

Nerden bilecektin bir öksüz olduğunu
Daha o anda, nerden

Öptüm yüzünü, gözünü
Uzaklaştım sonra bir kaçak gibi
Evimizden, mahalleden

Kaldığım odanın inik pancurlarını
Sert bir rüzgâr dövüyor şimdi
Küçük yüreğinde tanımsız kaygılar
Sen de beni düşünüyorsun belki

Uzun bir ayrılık var önümüzde
Aylarca, belki yıllarca sürecek olan
Ben ya tel örgüler arkasından
Bakacağım sana yine
Yüzünü, ellerini
Öpüp koklayamadan
Ya da uzakta, bir sürgünde
Sesinle yetineceğim sadece

Those songs I taped
With a dark presentiment
At home, but a day ago
Will you sing them to me once more
When we two meet again

Within me a tarry bitterness
An aching in my head
Only at the touch of your hands will it go;
Within me a tarry bitterness
A pitch-dark sorrow

If I only knew you wouldn't grow at all
That you would wait for me
With those songs you learned
With that four-year-old sweetness
I would endure the years-long agonies,
The prison and the exile

To me, of all the pains
Of all the separations
The one that most bitter seems
Is your growing up far away from me

From me, who wished to see
The burgeoning of your spirit, your body
Every tiny millimeter of you
As though nurturing a flower
With painstaking attention
In the warmth of my hands

Evimizde, bir gün önce
Karanlık bir önseziyle
Banda aldığım o türküleri
Yeniden karşılaştığımızda
Söyler misin bana yine

İçimde bir katran acılığı var
Başımda bir ağrı
Ancak senin elin dokunsa geçer
İçimde bir katran acılığı var
Zifir gibi bir keder

Bilsem senin büyümeyeceğini hiç
Bekleyeceğini beni
Öğrendiğin o türkülerle
O dört yaş şirinliğinle
Katlanırdım yıllar sürecek acılara
Hapise, sürgüne

Bana bütün acılardan
Bütün ayrılıklardan
Daha acı gelecek olan
Benden uzakta büyüyecek olman

Ben ki ruhunun, bedeninin
Her milimetreciğinin
Büyümesini görmek isterdim
Ellerimin sıcaklığında
Bir çiçeği
Büyütür gibi özenle

My little girl, my little girl, my little girl
No matter what comes, wait for your daddy to return
That he might love you
In your childhood just a little more

Oh long and
Mournful night
Oh
Love's aching bud . . .

Küçük kızım küçük kızım küçük kızım
Ne olur bekle dönüşünü babanın
Seni çocukluğunda
Biraz daha sevebilsin

Ey uzun ve
Ağıtlı gece
Ey
Acıyan tomurcuğu sevginin . . .

WHEN FACED BY LOVE

Know that all humanity is your friend, your sibling, my girl
Human beings are the product of joy, not of loathing, my girl
Hold your honor upright in the face of injustice
Bow down when faced by love, my girl

SEVGİNİN ÖNÜNDE

Bütün insanları dostun bil, kardeşin bil kızım
Sevincin ürünüdür insan, nefretin değil kızım
Zulmün önünde dimdik tut onurunu
Sevginin önünde eğil kızım

BABIES DON'T HAVE NATIONS

I felt this for the first time far from my homeland
Babies don't have nations
The way they hold their heads is the same
They gaze with the same curiosity in their eyes
When they cry, the tone of their voices is the same

Babies are the blossoms of humankind
Of roses the most pure, most the buds of roses
Some are fair fragments of light
Some are dusky-dark grapes

Fathers, do not let them slip your minds
Mothers, protect your babies
Silence them, silence them, don't let them speak
Who would talk of war and destruction

Let us leave them to grow up with passion
May they sprout and burgeon like saplings
They are not yours, nor mine, nor anybody's
They belong to the whole world
They are the apple of all humanity's eye

I felt this for the first time far from my homeland
Babies don't have nations
Babies are the blossoms of humankind
And our future's one and only hope

BEBEKLERİN ULUSU YOK

İlk kez yurdumdan uzakta yaşadım bu duyguyu
Bebeklerin ulusu yok
Başlarını tutuşları aynı
Bakarken gözlerinde aynı merak
Ağlarken aynı seslerinin tonu

Bebekler çiçeği insanlığımızın
Güllerin en hası, en goncası
Sarışın bir ışık parçası kimi
Kimi kapkara üzüm tanesi

Babalar, çıkarmayın onları akıldan
Analar, koruyun bebeklerinizi
Susturun, susturun, söyletmeyin
Savaştan, yıkımdan söz ederse biri

Bırakalım sevdayla büyüsünler
Serpilip gelişsinler fidan gibi
Senin, benim, hiç kimsenin değil
Bütün bir yeryüzünündür onlar
Bütün insanlığın göz bebeği

İlk kez yurdumdan uzakta yaşadım bu duyguyu
Bebeklerin ulusu yok
Bebekler, çiçeği insanlığımızın
Ve geleceğimizin biricik umudu

TURKEY, MY UNHAPPY LAND, MY LOVELY LAND

Turkey, my unhappy land, my lovely land
Sunflower with bowed neck
The future of poetry and love

Turkey, my unhappy land, my lovely land
Mountain wind, the honey of oranges
Humble, skillful, passionate

Turkey, my unhappy land, my lovely land
The bride whose fate is inscribed in black
The dried up milk in her breasts

Turkey, my unhappy land, my lovely land
Burning deep inside with a raging fire
Distressed in the hands of thieves

Turkey, my unhappy land, my lovely land
My wise and experienced land
The poets: Yunus, Pir Sultan, Nâzım

Turkey, my unhappy land, my lovely land
Folk songs, dirges, folk dances
Bread fresh from the oven

Turkey, my unhappy land, my lovely land
My mother, her face all wrinkled
My weeping pomegranate, smiling quince

TÜRKİYE, ÜZGÜN YURDUM, GÜZEL YURDUM

Türkiye, üzgün yurdum, güzel yurdum
Boynu bükük ay çiçeği
Şiirin ve aşkın geleceği

Türkiye, üzgün yurdum, güzel yurdum
Dağ rüzgârı, portakal balı
Alçak gönüllü, hünerli, sevdalı

Türkiye, üzgün yurdum, güzel yurdum
Yazgısı kara yazılmış gelin
Kurumuş sütü memelerinin

Türkiye, üzgün yurdum, güzel yurdum
Harlı bir ateş gibi derinde yanan
Haramilerin elinde bunalan

Türkiye, üzgün yurdum, güzel yurdum
Güngörmüş, bilge toprağım
Yunus, Pir Sultan ve Nâzım

Türkiye, üzgün yurdum, güzel yurdum
Bozlak, ağıt, halay ve zeybek
Dumanı üstünde ekmek

Türkiye, üzgün yurdum, güzel yurdum
Yüzü kırış kırış anam
Ağlayan narım, gülen ayvam

Turkey, my unhappy land, my lovely land
Sunshine on the grapevines
Deserving of the most beautiful future

Turkey, my unhappy land, my lovely land
Writhing beneath her chains
Beginning where they thought her done

Türkiye, üzgün yurdum, güzel yurdum
Asmaların üstünde gün ışığı
En güzel geleceğin yakışığı

Türkiye, üzgün yurdum, güzel yurdum
Zinciri altında kımıldayan
Bitecek sanıldığı yerde başlayan

IV   A SUMMER PAST

AUGUST GUEST

A flying insect came into my room for a moment
—Somewhat larger than a bee, with colorful wings—
It flew around a bit, without buzzing
Then it found its way to the window
And flew away

I was translating a Chekhov short story
A glass of beer on my table
—My room, my books, my ordinary world—
On the tulle curtains the sunbeams of August

It was a witness to my life
This flying insect, just for a moment
Then it flew away
So like a lover, who, for a moment,
Joins in my life, then disappears

AĞUSTOS KONUĞU

Odama bir an giren uçucu bir böcek
—Arıdan irice, kanatları renkli—
Dolaştı bir süre, vızıldamadan.
Sonra bulup yolunu pencerenin
Çıkıp gitti

Bir öykü çeviriyordum Çehov'dan
Masamda bira bardağı
—Odam, kitaplarım, olağan dünyam—
Tül perdede ağustos ışınları

Tanık oldu yaşamıma
Bu uçucu böcek, sadece bir an
Çıkıp gitti sonra
Tıpkı yaşamıma bir an katılan
Sonra yitip giden bir sevgili gibi

EVENING SORROW IN COUNTRY TOWNS

Evening sorrow in country towns
It's the same the whole world over
Clear blue sky and phantom houses
And the sad glances of women

Evening voices carried
By the wind from distant fields
The gradually darkening
Body of mountains in the evening

The childhood I spent in country towns
That gray melancholy of evening
Is for that reason close to my heart

For years I have lived with that melancholy
My nostalgia . . . oh how I yearn
To hear my mother call my name

TAŞRA KENTLERİNDE AKŞAM KEDERİ

Taşra kentlerinde akşam kederi
Her yerinde aynı dünyanın
Duru gök ve ev görüntüleri
Ve üzgün bakışı kadınların

Rüzgârın uzak kırlardan
Getirdiği akşam sesi
Dağların gecede git gide
Karanlıklaşan gövdesi

Taşra kentlerinde geçti çocukluğum
Akşamın o gri hüznü
Yakındır bu yüzden yüreğime

Yıllardır bu hüznü yaşıyorum
Hasretim nasıl da hasretim
Annemin adımı seslenişine

I'VE FORGOTTEN HOW MY MOTHER'S FACE LOOKED

I've forgotten how my mother's face looked
I've forgotten how my mother's voice sounded
Let nighttime be a blanket made of memories
Let me throw it over my black heart

I've forgotten how my mother laughed
I've forgotten how she was when she cried
Let life rock me in her arms
I am her tiny little son

I've forgotten how my mother's hands were
I've forgotten how her eyes were when she gazed
Let the wind bring the scent of dry grass
While the rain falls ever so gently

UNUTTUM, NASILDI ANNEMİN YÜZÜ

Unuttum, nasıldı annemin yüzü
Unuttum, sesi nasıldı annemin.
Gece bir örtü olsun anılardan
Kara yüreğime örtüneyim.

Unuttum, nasıldı annemin gülüşü
Unuttum, nasıldı ağlarken annem.
Yaşam sallasın kollarında beni
Küçücük oğluyum onun ben.

Unuttum, elleri nasıldı annemin
Unuttum, gözleri nasıldı bakarken.
Kuru ot kokusu getirsin rüzgâr
Yağmur usulcacık yağarken.

POEM ON THE THRESHOLD OF FORTY

From these minor enthusiasms, time out
Because the sun is my brother
I'm making love with a river
Because I'm the same age as the wind

To me, these days being calm,
Simplicity seems fitting
The beauty of poetry within
Competes with the joy of living

Oh, my life, more beautiful than beautiful
I'm falling hard for you increasingly
Woven with ever so much labor
I'm in a delicate, alluring embroidery

From these minor worries, attachments, time out
Because I'm the same age as the cosmos now
Without beginning, without end, insatiable
I am in a head-spinning flow

KIRK YAŞIN EŞİĞİNDE ŞİİR

Küçük heyecanlara paydos
Çünkü rüzgârla aynı yaştayım
Çünkü güneş kardeşim
Bir ırmakla sevişmekteyim

Bana artık dingin olmak
Bana yalınlık yaraşır
İçimde şiirin güzelliği
Yaşamak sevinciyle yarışır

Güzeller güzeli ömrüm
Sana gitgide sevdalanıştayım
Nice emeklerle dokunmuş
Bir ince, bir nazlı nakıştayım

Küçük tasalara, tutkulara paydos
Çünkü evrenle aynı yaştayım
Başsız sonsuz doyumsuz
Bir baş döndürücü akıştayım

IN PRAISE OF COWS

In my life I've seen so many cows
I must write for them a poem of praise
Cows lounging, strewn about the meadows
Cows endlessly musing as they graze

If I should call a woman cow-eyed
She'd consider it an insult, take offense
Yet the eyes of cows with melancholy gaze
Oh how beautiful those eyes and so immense

Returning from the pastures in the evening
So different from what other animals do
No jostling, no hubbub, no bells clanging
Just now and then perhaps a deep "moo"

They are a sign of great seriousness
That some things endure changelessly
Let this poem be a gift to cows
To their guarantee of stability

İNEKLERE ÖVGÜ

O kadar çok inek gördüm ki hayatımda
Onlara bir şiir adamam gerek
İnekler, yayılmış yatarlar çayırlarda
İnekler, sonsuzca otlayıp düşünerek

İnek gözlü desem bir kadına
Hakaret sayar bunu, gücenir
Oysa o mahzun bakışlı gözleri ineklerin
O iri gözleri nasıl da güzeldir

Akşamüstü otlaktan dönüşleri
Bir başkadır öteki hayvanlardan
Ne kargaşa, ne şamata, ne çıngırak sesi
Belki derin bir "mo" kimi zaman

Sonsuz değişmezliğin simgesidir onlar
Ve yüce bir ağırbaşlılığın
İneklere armağan olsun bu şiir
Güvencesine durağanlığın . . .

A SUMMER PAST

Yet another summer flowed away
Like water from my body seeping
In making love went the hours of day
And in white afternoons spent sleeping

What passed was just a summer
But the taste of salt is on my skin yet
And the fish we pulled out
With the evening sun from the same net

It was a summer in distant Georgia
On the shores of eagle mountains
That left a blue-eyed lake
In the dreams of children

It was a summer, its every second lived well
And the winds that from its sandy beaches whirl
Perhaps will chill a sea creature's shell
And remember a little girl

GEÇMİŞ YAZ

Gövdemden sızan sular gibi
Akıp gitti bir yaz daha
Sevişmelerle gündüz vakti
Ve beyaz öğle uykularıyla

Bir yazdı artık geçmiş olan
Oysa hâlâ tenimde tuz tadı
Aynı ağlardan çıkardığımız
Bir akşam güneşiyle balıkları

Bir yazdı uzak Gürcistan'da
Kıyısında kartal dağların
Mavi gözlü bir göl bırakan
Düşlerine çocukların

Bir yazdı yaşanan her saniyesi
Ve şimdi kumsaldan eserken rüzgâr
Üşür bir deniz kabuğu belki
Ve küçük bir kızı anımsar

ROSES AND MATH

Mathematics are lovely as a summer day
To solve a problem and profound roses
The problem deep within a rose
Is as lovely as a glass of water

My mother's laugh and a back garden
In a child's voice the problem and a rose
In the world's turning on a summer day
A problem seeks to equal a rose

GÜLLER, MATEMATİK

Matematik bir yaz günü kadar güzeldir
Derin güller ve bir problem çözmek
Bir gülün dibindeki problem
Bir bardak su güzelliğindedir

Annemim gülüşü ve bir arka bahçe
Çocuk sesinin içindeki problem ve gül
Dünyanın bir yaz günü dönüşünde
Bir problem bir güle eşit gibidir

IT WAS PARIS

It was Paris, night, and I was young
Thick and coal black flowed the Seine
I was high, was wet, was drunk
On love, on poetry, on pain

It was Paris, Paris of a thousand faces
Which was my beloved once upon a time
When September kissed my lips
One early evening as if to make them bleed

It was Paris, take sorrow over sorrows,
I wanted to die right there
I was dragging behind me
All of my unwritten poems

It was Paris, the Paris of my love
Every smile, each word a jar of secrets
As if I were all heart below to above
Shrouded in longing

It was Paris, the Paris of what time
Flying off with my fly-away life
Suddenly everything turned to memory
Love turned to lament

It was Paris, the Paris of night, of sorrow
Of the rain and of youth
Many thanks, for everything
That you withheld and offered

PARİSTİ

Paristi, geceydi, gençtim
Koyu simsiyah akıyordu Seine
Sarhoştum, ıslaktım, esriktim
Aşktan, şiirden, kederden

Paristi, binbir surat Paris
Bir zaman benim de sevgilim olan
Kanatır gibi bir akşamüstü
Öpünce eylül dudaklarımdan

Paristi, hüzünlerden hüzün beğen
Orada ölmek istiyordum
Yazılmamış şiirlerimi
Ardımsıra sürüklüyordum

Paristi, aşkımın Paris'i
Her gülüş, her söz bir sır küpüydü
Tepeden tırnağa bir kalptim sanki
Özleyişlerle örtülü

Paristi hangi zamanın Paris'i
Uçup giden yaşamla uçarak
Anıya dönüştü her şey birden
Ağıta dönüştü aşk

Paristi, gecenin hüznün Paris'i
Yağmurun ve gençliğin
Teşekkürler, esirgediğin
Ve sunduğun her şey için

YOU ARE MY BELOVED

You are my beloved, you have no time to think of who you are
       for thinking about what you need to do
One of the crowd in the midst of the crowd
A star, like a long-lost childhood, in the midst of night,
You are my beloved, I am kissing your teeth so white,
Hidden between them a half-line from last night's unfinished lovemaking

You are my beloved, my muffled love, my youth bleeding
Toward your childhood I set you flying
Your wings growing weary, you are drenched in sweat
Beside me, you wake in the night screaming
Mornings, I wave to your mingling with a metal life

You are my beloved, we stick a piece of paper in it and postpone our love
Which is lived furtively on buses and trains
Our bodies side by side unable truly to bleed

SEVGİLİMSİN

Sevgilimsin, kim olduğunu düşünmeye vaktin yok yapacak işleri
    düşünmekten
Kalabalığın içinde kalabalıktan biri
Gecenin içinde bir yıldız, yitip gitmiş çocukluk gibi
Sevgilimsin, ak dişlerini öpüyorum, aralarında bir mısra gizli
Dün geceki tamamlanmamış sevişmeden

Sevgilimsin, boğuk aşkım, kanayan gençliğim
Uçuruyorum seni çocukluğuna doğru
Kanatların yoruluyor, ter içinde kalıyorsun
Gece yanı başımda bağırarak uyanıyorsun
Her sabah el sallıyorum metalle karışmana

Sevgilimsin, arasına bir kâğıt koyup erteliyoruz aşkı
Otobüslerde ve trenlerde kaçamak yaşanan
Ve bedenlerimiz kana kana kanayamadan yan yana

LOVE IS A TWO-PERSON THING

The wind changes direction
Suddenly the leaves yellow;
The ship at sea loses its way
Vainly seeks a harbor;
The laugh of a stranger
Stole from you the one you love;
The poison accumulating inside you
Will only kill yourself
Death, one experiences alone
Love is a two-person thing

Not even a memory remains
Of making love the whole night long;
A thousand years far away
Is the skin you touched a thousand times;
The poems you would be able to write
Are long since written and done
Death, one experiences alone
Love is a two-person thing

They can't comfort you anymore
The old familiar songs;
Grief is freed from its chains
The waters flow backwards;
If you draw your love like a dagger
It will serve only to kill
The wild bird of passion
Up and flew away
Death, one experiences alone
Love is a two-person thing

AŞK İKİ KİŞİLİKTİR

Değişir yönü rüzgârın
Solar ansızın yapraklar;
Şaşırır yolunu denizde gemi
Boşuna bir liman arar;
Gülüşü bir yabancının
Çalmıştır senden sevdiğini;
İçinde biriken zehir
Sadece kendini öldürecektir;
Ölümdür yaşanan tek başına,
Aşk iki kişiliktir.

Bir anı bile kalmamıştır
Geceler boyu sevişmelerden;
Binlerce yıl uzaklardadır
Binlerce kez dokunduğun ten;
Yazabileceğin şiirler
Çoktan yazılıp bitmiştir;
Ölümdür yaşanan tek başına,
Aşk iki kişiliktir.

Avutamaz olur artık
Seni bildiğin şarkılar;
Boşanır keder zincirlerinden
Sular tersin tersin akar;
Bir hançer gibi çeksen de sevgini
Onu ancak öldürmeye yarar:
Uçarı kuşu sevdanın
Alıp başını gitmiştir;
Ölümdür yaşanan tek başına,
Aşk iki kişiliktir.

You're nothing but a lost melody
Played out and fallen from favor;
In your dreams a child sobs
As night rubs itself against the panes;
Because no butterfly
Experiences solitary passion
While loving, no insect,
No bird is alone
Death, one experiences alone
Love is a two-person thing

Yitik bir ezgisin sadece,
Tüketilmiş ve düşmüş, gözden.
Düşlerinde bir çocuk hıçkırır
Gece camlara sürtünürken;
Çünkü hiç bir kelebek
Tek başına yaşamaz sevdasını,
Severken hiçbir böcek
Hiç bir kuş yalnız değildir;
Ölümdür yaşanan tek başına,
Aşk iki kişiliktir.

10 POEMS ABOUT SEPARATION

I

We parted in life and death
Two bodies separated
Our hearts separated
Our voices separated, one from the other

Our hands separated
Our smells
Our waking up together in bed
Our laughing together
Our tears
Our dreams separated, one from the other

The dark night of the soul
Suddenly occluded everything

ON AYRILIK ŞİİRİ

I

Hayatta ve ölümde ayrıldık
Ayrıldı iki beden
Gönüllerimiz ayrıldı
Seslerimiz ayrıldı birbirinden

Ellerimiz ayrıldı
Kokularımız
Aynı yatakta uyanmalarımız
Gülüşlerimiz
Gözyaşlarımız
Düşlerimiz ayrıldı birbirinden

Ruhun içindeki gece
Kapladı her şeyi birden

II

Not just for the two of us
But for all of life, I'm sorry
In the photographs
The memory of a night

I am so much alone
It's like I'm dead
The old me is fading
And I can't become a new person

With amicable steps, sorrow
Comes and curls up with my heart
Life is serene
Like houses in the dawn

It's as if nothing at all happened
The two of us are just gone
There isn't any two of us anymore
The sea is always there
And the trees in their same dreams

II

Sadece ikimize değil
Bütün hayata üzgünüm
Fotoğraflarda
Bir gece hatırası

Öylesine yalnızım ki
Sanki yokum
Eriyor eski ben
Ve yeni biri olamıyorum

Keder sokulgan adımlarıyla
Gelip kıvrılıyor yüreğime
Hayat sakin
Şafakta evler gibi

Sanki hiç bir şey olmadı
İkimiz yokuz sadece
Biz olan ikimiz yokuz
Deniz hep orada
Ve ağaçlar aynı düşlerinde

III

The May morning sings its song in my heart
And the sound of a bird's wings
A bird's wing sound
The crying of a child

I am digging at the heart of the earth
Flowers gush forth and a May morning
I am digging at love
Agonies gush forth and unspoken words

Life calls out a challenge to me
And I am struggling anew to take hold of it
I am lying in wait
Taking aim with my sling

On a May morning, I'm a child
Not yet bruised, beautiful as green almonds
I am challenging life
With as yet unwritten poems

III

Mayıs sabahı kalbimde şarkısını söylüyor
Ve kanat sesleri bir kuşun
Bir kuşun kanat sesleri
Bir çocuğun ağlayışı

Kazıyorum yeryüzünün yüreğini
Çiçekler fışkırıyor ve bir mayıs sabahı
Kazıyorum aşkı
Acılar fışkırıyor, söylenmemiş sözler

Hayat bana meydan okuyor
Ve ben onu ele geçirmeye çalışıyorum yeniden
Tuzaklar kuruyorum
Sapanımla nişan alıyorum

Mayıs sabahları bir çocuğum ben
Örselenmemiş ve ilk çağla güzelliğinde
Hayata meydan okuyorum
Henüz yazılmamış şiirlerimle

IV

You'll become someone else, even if you don't want to
When another skin touches your skin
When your body connects with another body
Your breath mingles with another breath

You'll become someone else, even if you don't want to
While you're asleep at night or in the middle of the day
Without warning, you'll be startled by a feeling
As though you've stumbled on the brink of a precipice

You'll become someone else, even if you don't want to
Your clothes that bear traces of my gaze
Will exhaust their lives one by one
An armoire, a flower in the window, will change its place

You'll become someone else, even if you don't want to
A crease on your lip that came after me
A tone to your laughter that I don't really know
And your eyes that have already begun to forget me

And then, and then you are finally someone else

IV

Başka biri olacaksın istemesen de
Tenine başka bir ten dokunduğunda
Gövden buluştuğunda başka bir gövdeyle
Başka bir nefesle karıştığında nefesin

Başka biri olacaksın istemesen de
Gece uykunda ya da gün ortasında
İrkileceksin apansız bir duyguyla
Bir uçurum kıyısında sendelemiş gibi

Başka biri olacaksın istemesen de
Bakışlarımın izini taşıyan giysilerin
Tüketecek ömürlerini birer birer
Değişecek yeri bir dolabın, pencerede bir çiçeğin

Başka biri olacaksın istemesen de
Dudaklarında benden sonraki bir çizgi
Tanımadığım bir ton gülüşünde
Ve artık beni unutmaya başlayan gözlerin

Sonra, sonra artık başka birisin

V

Where the word ends
The heart begins to talk to itself
Some guy nails up a coffin
In the dim light of morning

Poetry
Begins where I start talking to myself
Like a candle
Starting to burn with a crackle

Of a morning, I
Seem to be in my childhood
If I don't stir
It seems that life will hold still

A vanishing love
Is like a vanishing childhood
Sorrow is stark naked on a summer noon
And casts no shadow

V

Sözün bittiği yerde
Yürek kendi kendine konuşmaya başlar
Tabut çiviliyor bir adam
Sabahın köründe

Şiir
Kendi kendimle konuştuğum yerde başlıyor
Bir mumun
Çıtırtılarla yanmaya başlaması gibi

Sabahleyin ben
Sanki çocukluğumdayım
Kımıldamasam
Hayat da duracak sanki

Yiten bir aşk
Yiten çocukluk gibidir
Hüzün çırılçıplaktır bir yaz öğlesinde
Ve gölgesizdir

VI

Past time
If remembered, is right now
Or else it's torn out and thrown away
Like a page from a notebook

What's torn out and thrown away
Can be a fluttering heart
Or else a summer night
Its stars dying in agony

VI

Geçmiş zaman
Anımsanıyorsa, şimdidir
Koparılıp atılır ya da
Bir yaprak gibi bir defterden

Koparılıp atılan
Çırpınan bir yürek olabilir
Ya da bir yaz gecesi
Yıldızları can çekişen

VII

Beneath my tongue there's longing
And a muddled plea
Drowned recollecting
Can't bring you back to me

Poems can't bring you back
Nor can a summer's leftover crumbs
If only I could have become a stone
Or sleep or wind

Springtime will again come along
Perhaps I will again be happy too
They'll resemble a mute singer's song
My happinesses after you

VII

Dilimin altında özlem var
Ve karışık bir dua
Boğulmuş anılar
Seni getiremez bana

Şiirler bana seni getiremez
Ne de bir yazdan kalan kırıntılar
Bir taş olabilseydim
Uyku ya da rüzgâr

İlkbahar yine gelecek
Belki yine mutlu olurum
Bir dilsizin şarkısına benzeyecek
Senden sonra mutluluğum

VIII

Like growing accustomed to a death
It will pass, the love we have for one another
A person doesn't have but one face
Nor a single destiny

When I sleep on a bed of stone
What pains me in the darkness
Is to think, without her I could still be

It is night, the damp voice of the wind
When it fills up my eyes with darkness
Summons the angel of hostility

VIII

Bir ölüme alışmak gibi
Geçecek birbirimize olan sevgimiz
İnsanın tek bir yüzü yoktur ki
Ya da tek bir geleceği

Taştan bir kutuda uyuduğumda
Beni acıtan karanlıkta
Düşünüp onsuz da olabileceğimi

Gecedir, rüzgârın ıslak sesi
Gözlerime karanlık dolduğunda
Çağırıp dargınlık meleğini

IX

Have a good death, sir, some midnight when a bleeding wind blows
Have a good death, where the deepest water flows

Let the acacia flowers grow purple and roses grow abundant
Have a good death, you springtimes past and present

A messy autumn comes, its eye sockets wet
A rain squall passes down the street barefoot

Have a good death, sir, may your mouth be sealed shut and eyes
For in a weary fall, with its bruises, it is good to die

IX

İyi ölümler bayım, rüzgârın kanadığı bir gece yarısında
İyi ölümler, en derin sularda

Morarsın akasya çiçekleri ve yoğunlaşsın güller
Geçmiş ve gelecek baharlara iyi ölümler

Gelir dağınık güz, göz çukurları ıslak
Geçer sokaktan bir yağmur yalnayak

İyi ölümler bayım, vurulsun ağzınıza ve gözlerinize mühür
Çünkü güz çürükleriyle iyi ölünür

X

A broken heart like shards of glass inside me
I close the pages of a worn-out book
Dusty sorrows, the taste of a faded smile

Now I am closing the pages of a worn-out life
Closing the doors of a bygone sea

X

İçimde cam kırıklarına benzeyen bir gönül kırıklığı
Kapatıyorum sayfalarını eskimiş bir kitabın
Tozlu hüzünler, solgun bir gülümseyiş tadı

Artık eskimiş bir hayatın sayfalarını kapatıyorum
Kapatıyorum geçmiş bir denizin kapılarını

IN A SUMMER ONCE, THEY HAD BURIED ME

In a summer once, they had buried me
In a stillness that might be anywhere
There was a woman on a balcony
With a wounded rose in her voice

Life and the seasons were the same thing
While drowning in waters deep as sleep
Springtime came along stuttering
From the children's shattered laughter

The sea was just over there and its mist
As voices dissolved in the air
A spell by all things cast
Mysterious scents, sounds of mirth

In a summer once, they had buried me
In a silence that was my mother
It was her heart that bloomed, maybe
Within a deep rose

BENİ BİR YAZA GÖMDÜLERDİ BİR ZAMAN

Beni bir yaza gömdülerdi bir zaman
Her yer olabilecek bir kuytulukta
Bir kadın vardı bir balkonda
Sesinde yaralı bir gül olan

Hayat ve mevsimler aynı şeydi
Uyku kadar derin bir suda boğulurken
İlkbahar kekeleyerek geldi
Kırık çocuk gülüşlerinden

Deniz oracıktaydı ve buğusu
Eriyorken havada sesler
Her şeyin bir büyü oluşturduğu
Gizemli kokular ve gülüşler

Beni bir yaza gömdülerdi bir zaman
Annem olan bir sessizlikte
Belki de onun kalbidir açan
Derin bir gülün içinde

IN SECRET MY BELOVED

Even dreams wait for nighttime
To appear in secret
You are in my heart, in the thing hidden within me
In secret my beloved

Let no one know how sorrowful I am
I carry this feeling around like my death
In my life's most secret, secluded spots
There's a place where my beloved sleeps, in secret

In secret, my beloved, bitter as life
Like the longing that fires my soul yet
I yearn in the depths of annihilation
For my beloved . . . in secret

GİZLİCE SEVGİLİM

Rüyalar bile geceleri bekler
Gizlice görünmek için
Yüreğimdesin, saklısında içimin
Gizlice sevgilim

Kimse bilmesin üzgünlüğümü
Taşırım ölümüm gibi bu duyguyu
En gizli kuytularında ömrümün
Bir yer var gizlice sevgilimin uyuduğu

Gizlice sevgilim, yaşam kadar acı
Canımı tutuşturan özlem gibi
Özlüyorum derin yok oluşta
Gizlice sevgilimi

V GAZEL TO A NEW LOVE

SPRINGTIME

I raised my face to the clouds
Murmuring as though in prayer
Washing myself with birds and grasses there
With the winds and springtime

The sun on my eyelids is warm
Ah! That fickle springtime sun
Is this real, or do I dream
I am here, or am not it seems

In a southern town, a coffeehouse by the shore
In waves, ears of grain endlessly roll
Here, alone with myself
This is how I can make my life whole

I have never kissed a bird on its tongue
Some day, perhaps, I can kiss one so
Some day, perhaps, I'll become a gust of wind
And across the ears of grain I'll blow
I want my heart to merge with a summer's day
In birdsong to be born anew

İLKBAHAR

Yüzümü bulutlara kaldırıp
Dua eder gibi mırıldanıyorum
Kuşlarla, otlarla yıkanıyorum
Rüzgârla, ilkbaharla

Güneş gözkapaklarımı ısıtıyor
O güvenilmez ilkbahar güneşi
Rüyada mıyım, gerçek mi bu
Hem var gibiyim, hem yok gibi

Bir güney kentinde, bir kıyı kahvesinde
Başakların sonsuz salınışı
Burada kendimle baş başa
Ömrümü böylece tamamlayabilirim

Bir kuşu dilinden hiç öpmedim
Belki bir gün öpebilirim
Belki bir gün rüzgâr olurum ben de
Eserim başakların üzerinden
Kalbim bir yaz gününe karışsın isterim
Bir kuş cıvıltısında doğmak için yeniden

THEY WERE EYES

They were eyes, that kindled with mute sorrow
They were eyes, that made useless the words

They were eyes, impassioned, tender, anxious
They were eyes, mother, lover, friend

They were eyes, in a child's innocence
Like a heart, throbbing

They were eyes, that while gazing on the world
Rendered it brilliant with meaning

They were eyes, that embraced me with glances
They were eyes, for which I now hopelessly long

They were eyes, that are no more
They were eyes, that are forever gone

They were eyes, the eyes of my childhood
Who knows in what worlds they now are

Perhaps, on the trail of glass beads
In a girl's braided hair

And the eyes of my early youth
Searching for the first poems

Chasing after the first passions
And cloudy dreams

GÖZLERDİ

Gözlerdi, tutuşan dilsiz bir kederle
Gözlerdi, gereksiz kılan sözcükleri

Gözlerdi, tutkulu, sevecen, kaygılı
Gözlerdi, arkadaş, anne, sevgili

Gözlerdi, çocuk masumluğunda
Ve bir yürek gibi atan

Gözlerdi, bakarken dünyaya
Onu anlamla aydınlatan

Gözlerdi, bakışlarıyla kucaklayan
Gözlerdi, umutsuzca özlediğim

Gözlerdi, şimdi arık olmayan
Gözlerdi, sonsuzca yitirdiğim

Gözlerdi, çocukluğumun gözleri
Şimdi hangi dünyalarda kim bilir

Saç örüklerinde bir kızın
Belki cam bilyelerin peşindedir

Ve ilk gençliğimin gözleri
Arayışında ilk şiirlerin

İlk sevdaların ardında
Ve bulutsu düşlerin

***

They were eyes, simply wishing
To believe that life must be deathless

They were eyes, tamely extinguished
Like a light in the darkness

They were eyes, that kindled with mute sorrow
They were eyes, mother, lover, friend

They were eyes, impassioned, tender, anxious
They were eyes, the eyes of those I loved

***

Gözlerdi, nasıl da inanmak isteyen
Yaşamın ölümsüz olduğuna

Gözlerdi, usulca sönüp giden
Bir ışık gibi karanlıkta

Gözlerdi, tutuşan dilsiz bir kederle
Gözlerdi, arkadaş, anne, sevgili

Gözlerdi, tutkulu, sevecen, kaygılı
Gözlerdi, sevdiklerimin gözleri

GAZEL TO A BYGONE SUMMER

Summer has passed, the sorrows remain
On lips the imprints of kisses remain

Over time the starry nights have grown sparse
Colder months and grayer days remain

Blackberry stains are wiped from fingers
Skinned and scabby knees remain

Of love's promises, of poetry
Fragments of verse, worn-out words remain

The birds migrated to the south in flocks
Behind them the sick and weak remain

Impatiens affronted, hydrangea miffed
Seas of a darkened blue remain

Summer has passed, but if passed, how long
In hearts bygone summers still remain

GEÇEN BİR YAZA GAZEL

Yaz geçti hüzünler kaldı
Dudaklarda öpüşlerden izler kaldı

Seyreldi gitgide yıldızlı geceler
Soğuk aylar, gri gündüzler kaldı

Böğürtlen lekesi silindi parmaklardan
Yarası kabuk bağlamış dizler kaldı

Aşk şiirlerinden, yeminlerden
Kopuk dizeler, kırık dökük sözler kaldı

Kuşlar göçtüler güneye sürülerle
Geride sayrılar, güçsüzler kaldı

Gücendi camgüzeli, ortanca küstü
Mavisi kararmış denizler kaldı

Yaz geçti, geçse de ne kadar
Gönüllerde geçmiş yazlar kaldı

GAZEL TO SOME WORDS

Words of summer that I pass
From notebook to notebook

Words, coy and flirtatious
Of love's first flutterings

Words only barely heard
Of a flower petal, a dewdrop

Words, all but noiseless
Of a snowflake strewn overnight

Words of a conjurer moon
The sun's words, frank, without deceit

Words, unforgettable
Of stars on a lonely night

Words, completely useless
In the wake of a bygone love

Words of joy and wild glee
That seek their own poetry

Words, momentous,
Of life, of love, and mortality

BAZI SÖZCÜKLERE GAZEL

Bir defterden bir deftere
Geçirdiğim yaz sözcükleri

İlk kıpırtılarında sevdanın
Eda ve naz sözcükleri

Taç yaprağının, çiğ damlasının
Duyulur duyulmaz sözcükleri

Geceye serpilen kar tanesinin
Gürültüsü az sözcükleri

Güneşin yalansız, dobra
Ayın sihirbaz sözcükleri

Bir yalnızlık gecesinde yıldızların
Unutulmaz sözcükleri

Biten bir aşk sonrasının
İşe yaramaz sözcükleri

Kendilerine şiirler arayan
Çılgınlık ve haz sözcükleri

Hayatın, aşkın ve ölümün
Olmazsa olmaz sözcükleri

A GAZEL TO HANDS

The hands I love are a woman's hands
The hands of oh-so-warm touchings

The hands of my mother or daughter
That make my dreams feather-light

The hands of my father, with whom I shared
The sorrows of our masculine destiny

The hands of my comrades
With whom I wove a lifetime

The hands of my loneliness
Clung to on so many solitary nights

The hands of partings and reunions
Our glances' inseparable companions

The hands of bards who put wings
To words and send them flying

The hands of that immortal love
I walk hand in hand with toward dying

ELLERE GAZEL

Sevdiğim eller bir kadının elleridir
Sımsıcak dokunuşlarının elleridir

Düşlerimi tüy gibi hafifleten
Annemin ya da kızımın elleridir

Erkek yazgımızın hüzünlerini
Paylaştığım babamın elleridir

Bir ömrü birlikte dokuduğumuz
Arkadaşlarımın elleridir

Nice yalnız gecede tutunduğum
Yalnızlığımın elleridir

Bakışlarımızın ayrılmaz yoldaşı
Ayrılmaların, kavuşmaların elleridir

Sözcüklere kanatlar takıp
Uçuran ozanların elleridir

Ölüme karşı el ele yürüdüğüm
Ölümsüz aşkın elleridir

THE EROTIC GAZEL

New passions purify me
Embracing till I go mad

Feet that I will cup in my palms
Like a pair of white carnations

Glances sparkling with desire
Lips trembling with mystery

Curls spilling onto alabaster shoulders
Beds unmade permanently

Garages, depots, airports
Reunions and separations

New passions purify me
New poems and going mad

EROTİK GAZEL

Beni yeni sevdalar paklar
Çıldırasıya sarılmaklar

Bir çift beyaz karanfil gibi
Avcumda tutacağım ayaklar

Tutkuyla ışıldayan bakışlar
Gizemle kıpırdayan dudaklar

Mermer bir omza dökülen bukleler
Toplanamayan yataklar

Garajlar, garlar, hava alanları
Kavuşmaklar ve ayrılmaklar

Beni yeni sevdalar paklar
Yeni şiirler ve çıldırmaklar

GAZEL TO A CHILD STANDING AT THE DOOR

The child standing at the door
Recalls a rustic vision

Sunshine kindles in her hair
In her eyes stirs an ocean

In the child standing at the door
All the ages are made complete

With a crackle mountains are born
The mighty oceans grow deep

Loves begin and come to an end
And the world keeps on turning

Night and day trail one another
In order, undeviating

The child standing at the door
Is unaware of any of these

From inside her and without
Life flows on without surcease

KAPININ ÖNÜNDE DURAN ÇOCUĞA GAZEL

Kapının önünde duran çocuk
Bir kır görünümünü andırıyor

Güneş tütüyor saçlarında
Gözlerinde bir deniz kımıldanıyor

Kapının önünde duran çocukta
Bütünleşiyor bütün zamanlar

Dağlar doğuyor çatırdayarak
Derinleşiyor okyanuslar

Aşklar başlıyor ve bitiyor
Dünya sürdürüyor dönmesini

İzliyor şaşmaz düzeninde
Gece ve gündüz birbirini

Kapının önünde duran çocuk
Habersiz bütün bunlardan

Hayat akıyor durmaksızın
Onun içinden ve dışından

GAZEL TO A LONG-AGO NIGHT

Suddenly, a long-ago night
Of its own accord in me born

The depot of a small town
And a motionless train

Everything sleeps, even the night
Only the stars are awake and I

Perhaps it is snowing persistently
Perhaps raining mistily

A song, just on the tip of my tongue
Made up of words forgotten now

Suddenly the cars move
A woman gazes from the window

A woman lost in dreams, pensive
A woman, looks at me without seeing

The cars pass, one after the other
The woman and train are lost to sight

Yet ever do I recall that night
Out of a thousand nights

BİR GEÇMİŞ ZAMAN GECESİNE GAZEL

Bir geçmiş zaman gecesi birden
Doğuyor içimde kendiliğinden

Bir küçük şehrin istasyonu
Ve kıpırtısız bir tren

Her şey uykuda, gece bile
Sadece yıldızlar uyanık ve ben

Belki kar yağıyor kesintisiz
Belki bir yağmur inceden

Dilimin ucunda bir şarkı
Şimdi unuttuğum sözcüklerden

Vagonlar kıpırdıyor ansızın
Bir kadın bakıyor pencereden

Bir kadın, düşler içinde, dalgın
Bir kadın, bakıyor beni görmeden

Vagonlar geçiyor birbiri ardına
Kadın ve tren yitiyor gözden

Artık hep o geceyi anımsıyorum
Binlerce gece içinden

GAZEL TO DEATH

Perhaps I've always thought secretly about death
In everything and before all else I thought of it

As though it were the identical twin within me
When I thought of myself, I thought of it

If now and again I appeared to have forgotten,
When I longed for forgotten things, I thought of it

When a girl in a thousand-year-old picture
Smiled sadly at me, I thought of it

In a dream where I encountered my unhappy childhood
As I ran my hands through her hair, I thought of it

I knew it was eyeing me from everywhere
I knew this and also thought of it

Although everyone is dying his own death
When someone died it was my death I thought of

My sense of life was so powerful that
Death was just a concept, I only thought of it

ÖLÜME GAZEL

Ölümü belki her zaman gizlice düşündüm
Her şeyin içinde ve her şeyden önce düşündüm

O benim içimdeki ikizimdi sanki
Onu kendimi düşününce düşündüm

Unutur gibi oldumsa da arada bir
Unuttuklarımı özleyince düşündüm

Bir tabloda bin yıl önceki bir kız
Bana kederle gülümseyince düşündüm

Üzgün çocukluğumla karşılaştım düşümde
Ellerini saçlarımda gezdirince düşündüm

Biliyordum her yerden beni gözlediğini
Bunu hep bildim ve sessizce düşündüm

Kendi ölümüyle ölüyorsa da herkes
Kendi ölümümü biri ölünce düşündüm

Öylesine güçlüydü ki yaşamak duygum
Bir kavramdı ölüm, onu sadece düşündüm

GAZEL TO A VANISHING LOVE

That summer sun which blinds my eyes
Turns into the image of a vanishing love

A sense of being lost that brings me hints of childhood
From the alienation within on desolate late afternoons

A traveler who's lost his way in a strange town
Who knows whence come and going whither

An echo that will never return to its voice
Repeating itself forlornly in the emptiness

Ever does that summer sun, that unconsoling sun above
Turn into the image of a vanishing love

YİTİP GİDEN AŞKA GAZEL

Hep o yaz güneşi, gözlerimi körleştiren
Bir aşkın imgesine dönüşüyor, yitip giden

Çocukluğumu anıştıran bir kaybolmuşluk duygusu
Issız akşamüstleri, içimdeki gurbetten

Yabancı bir kentte yolunu yitirmiş bir yolcu
Kim bilir nereden gelip nereye giden

Bir yankı, sesine dönmeyecek bir daha
Kimsesiz boşlukta kendini yineleyen

Hep o yaz güneşi, o avuntusuz güneş
Bir aşkın imgesine dönüşüyor, yitip giden

GAZEL TO A RIVER OF NIGHT

The river was flowing like a dark night
Writhing in the depths of the gorge

I gazed upon it from a hillock
My spirit flowing along with it

Its breast rose and fell
Illuminated by a frigid moon

How it was filled with itself alone
How oblivious it was and naked

Its song, the pain-filled song of the universe
Longing for freedom and yet imprisoned

River of night, brother of my spirit
It was flowing, colliding with its banks

GECE IRMAĞINA GAZEL

Kara gece gibi akıyordu ırmak
Dibinde uçurumun kıvrılarak

Ona bir tepeden bakıyordum
Ruhum onunla birlikte akarak

Göğsü kabarıyor alçalıyordu
Soğuk ayla aydınlanarak

Nasıl da kendiyle doluydu sadece
Nasıl da pervasız, çıplak

Şarkısı evrenin elemli şarkısıydı
Özgürlüğe özlemli ve tutsak

Gece ırmağı, kardeşi ruhumun
Akıyordu sınırlarına çarparak

GAZEL TO A NEW LOVE

I come to you crossing abysses
Crazy, flying I come to you

Forgetting what so often ended in grief
Oh so avidly I come to you

Full to overflowing with songs
Tongue-tied I come to you

My mind more jumbled than the bazaar
My heart all topsy-turvy I come to you

To learn everything all over again
To forget what I know, I come to you

Just like one newly come into the world
Stark naked and wailing I come to you

Saying, pluck me up again by the roots
So you'd set me flying, oh love, I come to you

YENİ AŞKA GAZEL

Uçurumlardan geçerek gelirim sana
Delice, uçarak gelirim sana

Unutup kederle biteni nice kez
Merak merak gelirim sana

İçim şarkılarla dolup taşarken
Dilim dolaşarak gelirim sana

Aklım bir pazar yerinden karışık
Gönlüm tepetaklak gelirim sana

Yeniden öğrenmek için her şeyi
Bildiklerimi unutarak gelirim sana

Dünyaya henüz gelenden farksız
Çığlık çığlık, çırıl çıplak gelirim sana

Kopar diye beni köklerimden yine
Uçur diye ey aşk, gelirim sana . . .

*A Brief Chronology of Significant Movements and
Cultural Trends in the History of Modern Turkey
and Turkish Poetry*

1789–1807 The reign of Sultan Selim III. Selim attempts to
modernize the organization of the military. *His spiritual
advisor and supporter, the Mevlevi dervish master Sheyh
Galip, writes his "Beauty and Love" verse narrative,
summing up the mystical tradition of Jalaluddin Rumi.
He faces the questions of how Ottoman spirituality,
thought, and literary culture are going to adapt to the
onset of a "modernizing" world.* A conservative reaction
by the Janissaries and their allies deposes the sultan, and
disbands the Nizam-i Cedid (New Order) army.

1808–1839 The reign of Sultan Mahmud II. The supporters of Selim
bring an army to Istanbul too late to prevent his execution
but they manage to put Mahmud II, another reform-
minded sultan, on the throne. Mahmud's early attempts
at reform are blocked by reactionary elements allied with
the Janissaries.

1826 Mahmud accomplishes the massacre of the Janissaries in
Istanbul and the disbanding of Janissary units all over
the empire. The beginning of a reform of Ottoman
institutions, including the opening of a "translation
office"—which trained Ottoman officials in foreign
languages—an educational reform, and a restructuring
of the bureaucracy.

1839   The Royal Rescript of the Gülhane officially initiates
            the beginning of the Tanzimat (Reorderings/Reforms)
            period (1839–1876), in which major governmental
            reforms, many based on European models, are instituted.

1859   *Publication of İbrahim Şinasi's translations from French
            poetry. A period of literary experimentation based on
            European models (the literary Tanzimat) begins 1859–
            1860 under the leadership of Namık Kemal, Ziya Paşa,
            and İbrahim Şinasi. They attempt to merge a Turkish/
            Muslim spirit with the sensibility and freedom of European
            literature and experiment with new forms: novels, plays,
            free verse poetry. Poets are engaged in turning away from or
            reinterpreting the old Ottoman forms, rhythms, themes, and
            vocabularies. Major literary figures travel to Europe. They also
            discuss their views in published works and newspaper articles.*

1876–1909 The reign of Abdülhamit. An Ottoman constitution
            is promulgated.

1877   The opening of the Ottoman parliament.
(March)

1878   The end of the reform period and the beginning of autocratic
(February) rule under Abdülhamit. The parliament is dismissed and
            the constitution is suspended. *From 1877 to 1884, Namık
            Kemal is exiled to the island of Midilli. In 1879, Abdülhak
            Hamit's vastly influential poetry collection* Sahra *(The
            Wilds) is published.*

1880–1896 *The era of the so-called Ara Nesli (Interim Generation),
            a diverse group of writers and poets who grew up and were
            educated under the influence of the Tanzimat reforms. They*

engage in spirited debates on such topics as the old and new literatures, romanticism and naturalism, what poetry is, who can be called a poet, literary theory and literary criticism, etc.

1896   *The poet Tevfik Fikret takes over editorship of the influential literary journal* Servet-i Fünun *(Riches of the Arts), whose writers variously come to reflect in their work both a response to and escape from the malaise of a country demoralized by defeats, economic crisis, severe censorship, and autocratic rule. Their language becomes more obscure under the influence of European symbolism and impressionism, their themes become more melancholy, their worldview often reflects a world that seems empty and without hope.*

1901   *The journal* Servet-i Fünun *is closed by order of the sultan.*

1902–1912 *The era of the Fecr-i Ati (Coming Dawn) school of poets and writers. They continue exploring the future of the new Ottoman literature, following the path laid down by the Servet-i Fünun school. The turn of the century will also see the rise of other movements, such as the Neo-Hellenic (Nev-Yunaniler) movement, which sought to find Western and Central Asian bases for the renaissance of a Turkish literature freed from the influences of Arabic and Persian. The impact of some of these movements will be quite long-lasting as they join the tide of Turkish nationalist literature in the 1930s and beyond.*

1908   The Ottoman Third Army revolts in Salonika. Abdülhamit is forced to restore the Constitution of 1878.

1909   Abdülhamit is deposed by the Third Army, whose officers form the core of the Committee of Union and Progress.

idea of Turkishness are advanced by Halide Edip Adıvar, Yakup Kadri Karaosmanoğlu, and others.

1930s   *A period of intense development with regard to modern Turkish poetry, punctuated by debates about form, rhythm, language purification, and the relation between modern poetry and the poetry of the Ottoman past. There is a focus on creating a Turkish "national" literature, often conceived of as derived from a continuous history of purely "Turkish" culture descended from Central Asian roots, existing apart from and untainted by "Ottoman" culture. While the socialist poet Nâzım Hikmet starts another movement against traditional poetic formulations, Yahya Kemal Beyatlı reinvents old poetic media to express nationalist and nostalgic themes.*

1934   Mustafa Kemal takes the name Atatürk. Family names are required of all citizens.

1938   Atatürk dies. İsmet İnönü is chosen as president, and leader of the Republican People's Party. Nâzım Hikmet is arrested and begins twelve years in prison.

1939–1945 The Second World War. Turkey remains neutral.

1940   *The founding of the Village Institutes (Köy Enstitüleri), which brought educated, often urban, individuals to Turkish villages, where they were expected to promulgate the ideals of the new Turkey—a project which, at the least, educated many urban elites on the lives of village people and promoted a literary interest in Turkish villagers. The Institutes were the successors of the Folk Houses (Halkevleri), which published many magazines of poetry and prose written by villagers.*

1940s   *The development of socialist realist poetry, which drew on both Western realist poetry and the folk poetry of rural Turks. [İlhami Bekir Tez (1906–1984), Hasan İzzettin Dinamo (1909–1989), Rıfat Ilgaz (1911–1993)]. Literature becomes more reactionary.*

1941   *Orhan Veli (Kanık), Melih Cevdet (Anday), and Oktay Rifat (Horozcu) publish their poems and an influential manifesto in the volume entitled* Garip *(Bizarre), which initiates the Garip movement, later called the Birinci Yeni (First Renewal or First New). Their goal was to introduce modernism into Turkish poetry in a systematic way that included the use of common spoken language, literal imagery, and ironic attacks on both the neo-Ottoman poetry of their day and the hyper-seriousness of socialist realism.*

1942   *Ataol Behramoğlu is born in Çatalca.*

1943   *Necip Fazıl publishes the journal* Büyük Doğu *(The Great East) and espouses a conservative modernism with a basis in mystical Muslim spirituality.*

1946   The Democratic Party is founded as an opposition party.

1950   The Democratic Party wins the election and, under the Prime Minister Adnan Menderes, replaces İnönü's Republican People's Party. *In a general amnesty, Nâzım Hikmet is released, and the next year flees Turkey. The Council of Ministers rescinds his Turkish citizenship.*

1950s   *The Hisar Dergisi (The Castle Journal) group argues that, in order to rescue poetry from its modernist rootlessness and*

*restore poets to their rightful degree of respect, there should
be a return to set forms, rhyme schemes, and rhythms.*

1951–1952 The religious Imam-Preacher Schools are reopened.

1952 The Village Institutes are closed.

1954 *A socialist realism controversy emerges in literary circles
after the publication of a series of articles on the topic by the
poet Attilâ İlhan in* Mavi *(Blue), a literary magazine. The
ephemeral so-called Mavi movement is born.*

1955 *The beginning of the movement that will come to be called
the İkinci Yeni (Second Renewal or Second New). It was a
complex response to social, political, and literary trends,
which, among other things, was more open to the Ottoman
past, tended toward a surrealistic style without claiming
to be surrealist, and reintroduced experimentation with
imagery in contrast to Garip's austerity. The writers of the
Second Renewal focused on poetry for its own sake and did
not appear to have an overall political program, nor did they
belong to a political movement, which made their poetry
seem strange and even obscure to many of their readers
who had come to expect a political agenda and a political
interpretation of poetry.*

1959–1960 University student uprisings against the Democratic Party,
followed by a military coup that removes the Democratic
Party government from office and arrests its leaders.

1960 *Sezai Karakoç founds the influential literary magazine* Diriliş
*(Revival), which will play a leading role in the development of
modernist Islamicist poetry.*

1960–1970 Papirüs Dergisi *(The Papyrus Journal), edited by the poet Cemal Süreya, publishes articles advocating new approaches to the criticism of contemporary literature.*

1961 İsmet İnönü leads a transitional government. A new constitution is promulgated.

1961 *The first edition of Yahya Kemal Beyatlı's (1884–1958) poetry collection* Kendi Gök Kubbemiz *(Our Own Dome of Sky) is published, followed the next year by* Eski Şiirin Rüzgariyla *(On the Wind of Ancient Poetry).*

1963 *Nâzım Hikmet dies in Moscow. His work has been published in many languages for many years but only following his death is it published in Turkey.*

1965 The Justice Party, an offspring of the Democratic Party, wins the elections and forms a government under Süleyman Demirel.

1965 *Behramoğlu's first collection of poems is published.*

1966 *Nâzım Hikmet's* Memleketimden İnsan Manzaraları *(Human Landscapes from My Country) is published in Turkey.*

1968–1972 Revolutionary Marxist and leftist university youth begin protesting and are harshly put down by the police and military. The military issues a warning and several left-leaning public organizations are closed, including the Turkish Workers' Party.

1970–1974 *Behramoğlu lives in Paris, where he meets Pablo Neruda and Louis Aragon.*

1975–1977 *Behramoğlu edits the journal* Militan *(The Militant).*

1978–1980 *The journal* Sanat Emeği *(The Labor of Art) is published by Ataol Behramoğlu, Turgay Fişekçi, Orhan Taylan, and Barış Pirhasan.*

1980s *Emergence of a new trend in Turkish poetry featuring imagist characteristics after the style of Attilâ İlhan—for example, in the poetry of Murathan Mungan. The number of published women poets increases dramatically.*

1980 A military coup closes all political parties and civil organizations.

1982 A new Turkish constitution is promulgated. *The activities of leftist politicians and artists are harshly repressed. Ataol Behramoğlu is arrested in March with other executive members of the Turkish Peace Society and spends eight months in a military prison. He receives the Lotus Prize of the Afro-Asian Writers' Association while in prison. In 1983 he is sentenced to eight years in prison and thirty-two months of internal exile for his activities with the Turkish Peace Society. He flees the country and lives in exile in Paris until 1989, when his sentence is commuted.*

1983 Üç Çiçek *(Three Flowers), recognized as the most important literary journal of the 1980s, is published irregularly. The journal defends "art for art's sake" in the spirit of the Second Renewal.*

1986 Şiir Atı *(The Poetry Horse), a very important but irregularly published literary jorunal of the 1980s, joins* Üç Çiçek *in arguing in favor of art for art's sake and against the politicization of poetry.*

1988   *Küçük İskender's* Gözlerim Sığmıyor Yüzüme *(My Eyes Don't Fit in My Face) starts the fashion of "marginal poetry," which experiments with jazz and rap rhythms in order to give voice to marginal lifestyles, discussions of public space, and subcultural movements such as the feminist movement, Green movement, gay movement.*

1990–1999 Sombahar Dergisi *(Autumn Journal) and* Ludingirra, *published by Orhan Kahyaoğlu, become influential sources of contemporary poetry and criticism. While not themselves Islamist, these journals did not reject Islamist writing out of hand.*

1990–1991 The Gulf War.

1997   On February 28, the so-called postmodern military coup closes the populist-conservative Welfare Party (Refah Partisi) without actual military intervention by announcing its intentions in an Internet environment.

2003   U.S. and coalition forces invade Iraq.

2004   *The bi-monthly* Yasak Meyve *(Forbidden Fruit) publishes special features on the emerging movement of Kurdish poets writing in Turkish.*

2006   Orhan Pamuk wins the Nobel Prize.

1913   The Committee of Union and Progress takes over the government.

1918   The Allied fleet arrives in Istanbul.

1919   The Greeks land in Izmir, claiming it and parts of Anatolia. The Turkish National Congress meets in Erzurum. Mustafa Kemal arrives in Samsun.

1920   A provisional Turkish government is established in Ankara.

1921   The Grand National Assembly in Ankara adopts the Fundamental Law. The battle of Sakarya; the Turks defeat the Greeks. The French and the Italians agree to withdraw from Turkey.

1922   Mustafa Kemal abolishes the sultanate.

1923   Ankara becomes the capital of Turkey. The Republic of Turkey is proclaimed.

1924–1928   The caliphate is abolished. Wearing the fez is prohibited. Turkey is declared a secular state. The Latin alphabet is adopted. Subsequently, the religious endowments are taken over by the state, the dervish cloisters are closed, and the dervish orders are banned. The Turkish Language Academy and History Academy are founded to facilitate the reform and purification of the Turkish language and the writing of a history of the Turkish nation. *Within a generation, Ottoman literature will become inaccessible to all but a small cadre of specialists. The nationalist novel genre and engaged literature flourish. Highly political ideas that help form a particular*